PHOTOGRAPHING
PEMBROKESHIRE

A PARADISE FOR PIRATES

This book is dedicated to my wife, Jo,
who has been alongside me for 32 years
and who accompanied me without complaint
on most of my photo shoots, particularly
when I deviated off the beaten track;
to our daughter Bridie, always observant,
who continually keeps me on my toes;
and to our two loving grandchildren,
Dylan and Efan – our pride and joy.

PHOTOGRAPHING
PEMBROKESHIRE

A PARADISE FOR PIRATES

IEUAN MORRIS

First impression: 2021
© Ieuan Morris & Y Lolfa Cyf., 2021

The publishers wish to acknowledge the support of the
Books Council of Wales.

Cover design: Y Lolfa
Design: Y Lolfa & Richard Huw Pritchard
Cover image and all other images: © Ieuan Morris
except p.17: Orem (Wikimedia Commons CC BY-SA 3.0)

ISBN: 978-1-78461-754-7

Published and printed in Wales on paper from
well-maintained forests by Y Lolfa Cyf., Talybont,
Ceredigion SY24 5HE

e-mail ylolfa@ylolfa.com
website www.ylolfa.com
tel 01970 832 304
fax 832 782

Contents

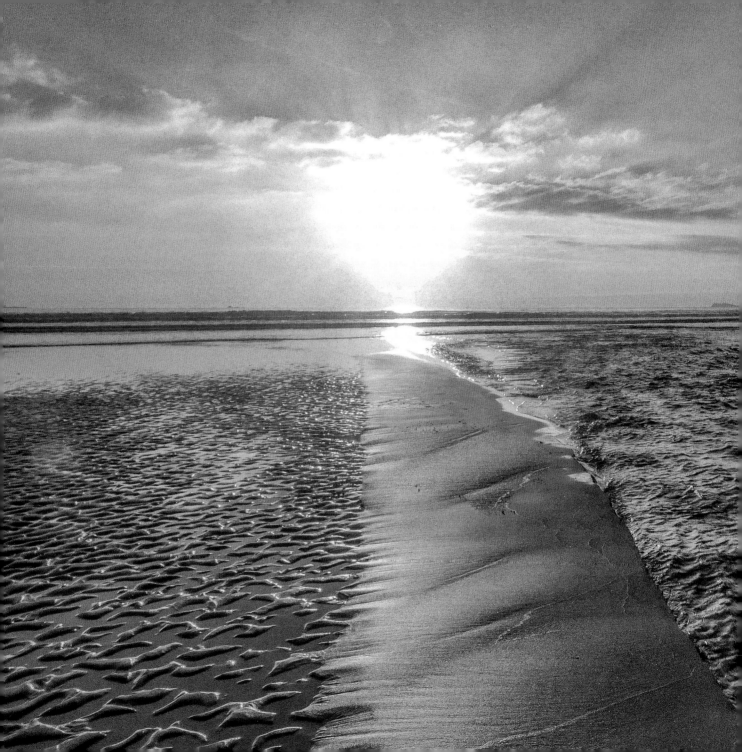

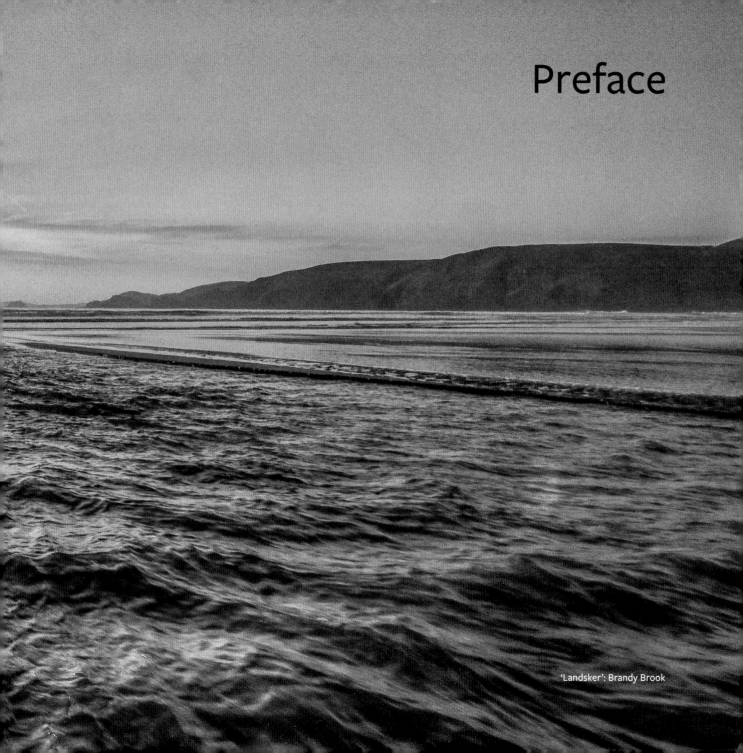

Preface

'Landsker': Brandy Brook

I HAVE ALWAYS retained a strong attachment to Pembrokeshire (Sir Benfro), the county where I was born, and its places. It is where I lived and grew up before seeking a further education beyond these shores and a career in Law, firstly in London and then for almost 40 years as a barrister in Cardiff.

I have in recent times put away the law reports, interpretation of statutes and intricate rules of evidence that once occupied my professional life. As interesting and rewarding as practice at the Bar has been, I have now hung up my well-worn wig and ragged gown and rekindled my keen interest in photography. These days, equipped with camera, lens and tripod against the spectacular scenery that this magnificent coastline provides, I have been inspired to retread long-familiar territory to capture in photographic form that which has always astounded me.

The county of Pembrokeshire, with its striking coastline and exciting hinterland, both rich in history and character, have over the years attracted both artist and photographer and provided them with endless opportunities to record landscape, nature and wildlife. It is quite unrivalled in many ways. Its solitude and beauty also provide a great retreat to writer and poet, and the unique light that this corner of south-west Wales has to offer has inspired directors of both film and television to select areas of the county as a backdrop for their work. Pembrokeshire itself can claim credit over many years for producing its own distinguished catalogue of painters and eminent artists, as well as attracting many others from all over the globe who have settled in the area.

Pembrokeshire is a county located on the most westerly extreme of Wales, with a land area of just over 600 square miles – five times larger than Malta, and slightly smaller than Tenerife. It has a permanent resident population of around 125, 000 and a high number of holiday homes. In fact, Pembrokeshire County Council has recently imposed a 50% levy on the annual council tax for this category of homeowner, thereby penalising absentee 'occupiers'.

The Pembrokeshire Coast Path, which has been designated as a national trail, is 186 miles in length and was opened on 16 May 1970 by Wynford Vaughan-Thomas, then Chairman of the Council for the Preservation of Rural Wales. It was very much inspired by the painstaking research of Ronald Lockley (1903–2000), Welsh ornithologist and naturalist, and offers some of the most spectacular and rugged coastal scenery in Britain.

The Coast Path runs from St Dogmaels (Llandudoch) in the north to Amroth in the south and its whole length is almost entirely contained within the Pembrokeshire Coast National Park. Established in 1952 with an area of 240 square miles, it is unique as Britain's only coastal national park. The emblem that appears upon national park signage is the razorbill. They, like thousands of seasonal visitors, are attracted to the county. Around 12,000 of this species of seabird annually invade Skomer Island (Ynys Sgomer), where they only land to breed. After breeding, the razorbill will winter in the North Atlantic.

In 2010, National Geographic recognised Pembrokeshire as one of the top-rated coastal destinations in the world, having 'a magnificent protected coastline from both ecological and geological perspectives... with a very established tourism industry.' And in August 2019, Lonely Planet named the Pembrokeshire Coast National Park one of the top ten ultimate travel experiences in the UK, describing it as a 'ravishing stretch of cliff-flanked coves, thrashing seas, wildflower-freckled moors and hedge-rowed tracks leading to one-pub villages'.

Living here has given me an intimate knowledge of the county's geography, its peoples, their customs and traditions. Many of the indigenous people have remained, never leaving the comfort of their community and the spirit it traditionally aroused. A number of those have become characters in their own right, many of whom I have photographed for this book. A percentage, such as myself, left the area for a variety of reasons, only to return.

My aim throughout this book was to photograph and capture locations where past events of notoriety have taken place, accompanying the image with a descriptive text. The images I have taken do not always tread the path of the familiar hotspots seen by photographers, and I have not dared to embark on the preserve of the dexterous wildlife photographer.

When I started to write about these events, I focused upon the seafarers and raiders who regularly plundered the coast of Pembrokeshire between the seventeenth and eighteenth centuries. From earliest times, the county of Pembrokeshire and its seaboard of St George's Channel and the Celtic Sea have been persistently plagued with an insatiable greed for wrecking, smuggling, raiding and acts of piracy. I quickly realised, however, that to limit my research into the invasion of the county to such a restricted period would be to close my eyes to the intrusive activities of others present here much earlier, and those that continue relentlessly to descend upon this corner of Wales to this day. Those considerations caused me to revisit occurrences either side of that original time span, and to dwell upon related and perhaps more significant matters that have shaped the county and account for it being distinctive in many ways. Whether Viking, Elizabethan privateer, smuggler, wrecker, modern-day trafficker in controlled drugs or powerful commercial

entity, each alike has seized upon the seclusion of the county and the deep and treacherous waters that provide cover and shelter to a long rugged coastline.

My research has provided me with the inspiration for this book and the incentive to photograph what I consider to be a range of subjects that may be of interest to both visitor and local alike. Whilst not seeking to provide a detailed, in-depth analysis – which has been offered elsewhere – I have given prominence to some of the locations frequented by pirates, smugglers, wreckers and others who have discovered the county and exploited the coastline. I have tried to ensure that the detail in the stories is factually accurate, though in some instances it has no doubt been embellished in the telling over the years.

Discovering this jewel and its environs has brought a horde of visitors to the county by land, sea and air, both welcome and unsought, which has alerted the native population and law enforcement agencies to be on guard to protect our fragile habitat and treasured coastline. The English essayist and literary critic Samuel Johnson, as long ago as 1773, made this astute observation about 'discovery' in general and its potential detrimental consequences: "I do not much wish well to discoveries, for I am always afraid they will end in conquest and robbery."

The insidious threat of industrial pollution is but one contemporary issue which, if unabated, is potentially detrimental to the environment and to tourism, and to the county itself. The conflict between unscrupulous exploitation by large corporate bodies and the importance of ecological considerations has caused the Government and the planning authorities to wrestle with their consciences against conditions of civil disobedience. The emergence of Extinction Rebellion (XR) in May

2018 and the peaceful occupation of prominent sites throughout the country since then in order to compel the Government into taking action on climate change and biodiversity loss is very much a controversial issue.

As well as having a flourishing tourist industry that seems to grow annually, the county has experienced an influx of peoples relocating permanently to Pembrokeshire for socio-economic reasons not just from other parts of the United Kingdom, but 'invading' from all over the globe. This is not without precedent. There were early incursions by the Vikings (the Old English term *wicing* meant 'pirate' or 'raider'), who sailed from Scandinavia through the dense fogs of the North Sea to attack our shores, before settling and leaving a legacy of place names accompanied by a simultaneous dissemination of Norse culture through the area.

The Norman Conquest and their later efforts to conquer Wales created a frontier of castles dissecting north and south, thereby forming a 'line' from the west coast to the southeast coast of the county – from Newgale (Niwgwl) at Brandy Brook, across to Roch (Y Garn), Haverfordwest (Hwlffwrdd), Narberth (Arberth) and Amroth. The subsequent settlement of the area to the south of this line by the Flemish brought a language different to that spoken by the native peoples. The Welsh inhabitants in the north successfully rebelled against colonisation, and the language spoken to the north of what has become known as the Landsker Line is predominantly Welsh. Those living 'down below' (south of the Landsker) speak an idiom which borders on that spoken in the south-west of England. I have lived both north and south of this unusual and unique divide, and what exists on either side of it was traditionally very different both linguistically and culturally. In addition to the many curious distinctions, the landscape and stunning coastline both have very different aspects, which I have attempted to reflect through my photography.

George Owen of Henllys, the Welsh Elizabethan antiquarian, wrote in the seventeenth century of those living in the south of Pembrokeshire:

> "(They) keep their language among themselves without receiving the Welsh speech or learning any part thereof, and hold themselves so close to the same that to this day they wonder at a Welshman coming among them…"

It is no coincidence that the place names below the Landsker are also not Welsh – to the extent that, over the centuries, South Pembrokeshire has acquired the curious epithet, 'Little England beyond Wales'.

A tourist passing through the county from north to south may be truly perplexed by such bizarre differences. For instance, encountering the quaint Welsh-speaking village of Llandissilio (named after seventh-century Welsh saint Tysilio) in the north, before stopping just a few miles south and being served a traditional 'English high tea' without a trace of the Welsh language in the village of Bosherston (Llanfihangel-clogwyn-Gofan) may seem odd. Continuing to travel north-west across the River Cleddau and staying overnight, for instance, at Llanungar outside the village of Solva (Solfach) could be even more mystifying. This curious hybrid name is a fusion of the Welsh *llan*, referring to church grounds, and the Viking-derived *Unga*.

For political, economic and environmental reasons, the county in some respects remains remote and at times isolated. Resisting any further incursion beyond Pont Abraham from the M4 motorway, the railway system fares no better, with Swansea (Abertawe) High Street Station being the last bastion before the stop-start debacle to

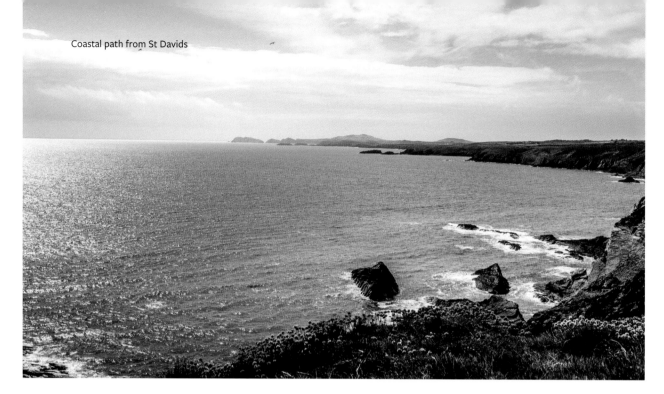

Coastal path from St Davids

the west: some trains going no further than Carmarthen (Caerfyrddin). The further west, the more cut off things become. Back in the twelfth century, Gerald of Wales described the area between Newgale and St Davids as bleak in the extreme, and as being "swallowed up by the violence and the encroachments of the sea".

Those characteristic features of seclusion and relative tranquillity, together with the more obvious virtues that the county has to offer, have, however, proved on balance to be a positive attraction to others. Many regard Pembrokeshire today as a place to go to throughout the year, a prime tourist destination free of the irritating airport delays and associated hindrances that can often accompany travel overseas.

Further, for those who were, in pre-Covid times, absorbed in the repetitive routine of city life and longed for a break from the everyday commute to their desk, a rushed sandwich at lunchtime and the long trudge home again at night, the county has provided both relaxation and a healthy inspiration in a world far removed from what is sometimes a humdrum existence. For others bent on achieving 'the good life', the break can have the consequence of being a permanent move, going beyond a welcome weekend visit or an annual vacation, many showing a determination to integrate and to make a positive contribution to the community in which they have come to settle. The advent of the Internet and improved communication can also mean that a successful business venture can be conducted from home whcrever that may be considered desirable – as has been amply demonstrated over the last couple of years – and Pembrokeshire is proving to be just that.

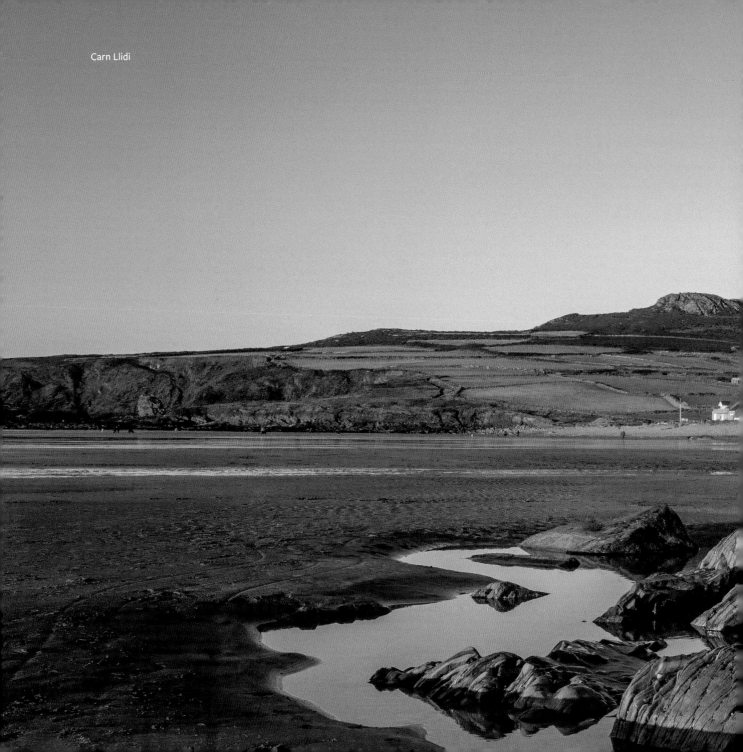
Carn Llidi

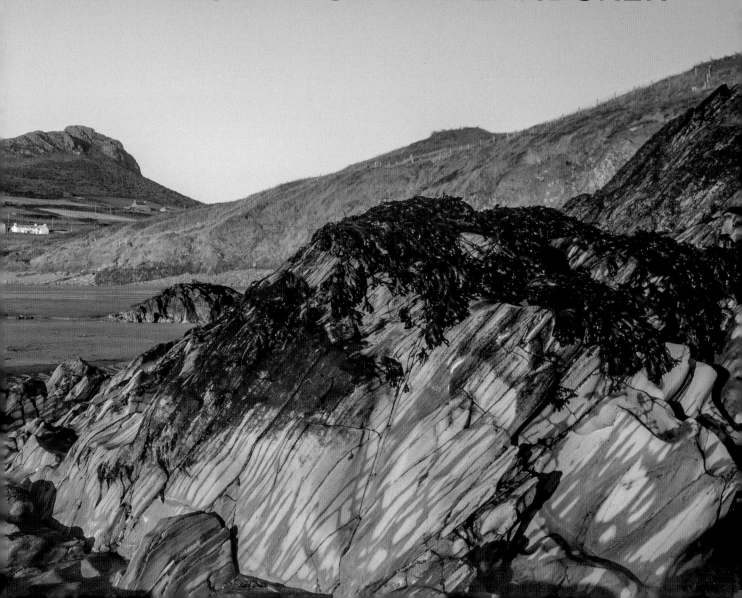

SECTION 1
NORTH OF THE LANDSKER

CASNEWYDD BACH

Yn y pentref yma y ganed

BARTI DDU

y môr-leidr enwog.
(1682-1722)

In this village the famous
pirate Black Bart was born.

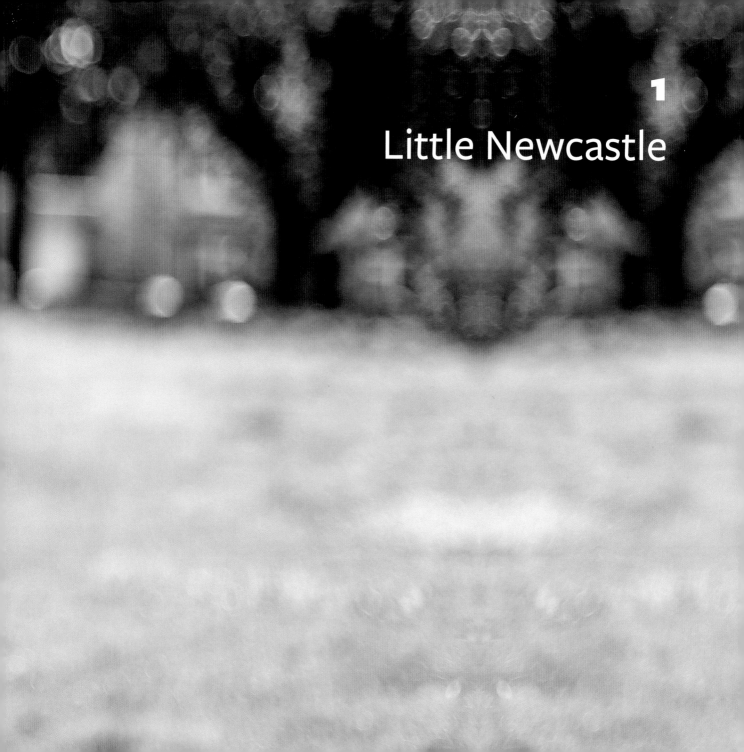

Little Newcastle

The greatest and most lethal – that was Roberts

INCONGRUOUS AS IT may sound, my starting point on this photographic voyage is a locality that some may consider, on the face of it, an insignificant place some seven miles from the sea, where there was no piracy, smuggling, wrecking or invasion. However, it is the birthplace of the greatest of all pirates: Bartholomew Roberts. His infamy and strict regard for discipline amongst his crew placed him way above his contemporaries, and has since focused attention on Little Newcastle (Casnewydd Bach). Consequently, there are no scenic coastal images to pore over, and instead I have chosen to devote a little more time to dwelling upon some of the detail surrounding this fascinating character.

John Roberts (1682–1722), more commonly known as Bartholomew Roberts or 'Barti Ddu' after his death, was ranked by many during the Golden Age of Piracy as the 'most lethal of pirates', reputedly capturing over 400 ships and £80 million of treasure. Little Newcastle is a small village situated between Letterston (Treletert) and Puncheston (Casmael), near the Preseli foothills in North Pembrokeshire, thousands of miles from the Caribbean, where Roberts gained his notoriety on the high seas. Though his place of birth was inland, he had easy access to the sea, and it is believed that at the age of 13 he left the area and served aboard merchant ships, gaining vast experience on slavers and ending up as third mate. In June 1719 off West Africa, he was taken aboard ship as a reluctant recruit by a pirate captain who, coincidentally, was also a Pembrokeshire man from Milford Haven: Hywel Davies. After the demise of Hywel Davies in the same year, Roberts was chosen as new leader and captain. This was a remarkable achievement within mere months of being made a mate. For the son of a poor farmer from an isolated Welsh village, his reputation and exceptional character has provided a worldwide legacy that remains intriguing to this day.

His knowledge of the seas, shrewdness and cunning were qualities that were to make him the greatest of all pirate captains. He soon gained infamy, amassing considerable wealth from his activities in Brazil, the Caribbean and West Africa. So successful was this Pembrokeshire-born pirate that he was the scourge of the Atlantic and the Caribbean during the years 1719–21.

He also designed his own flags, which flew from his flagship, the *Royal Fortune*, captured from the French. On one flag, Roberts is shown in white with a sword in hand, on a black background on two skulls labelled 'ABH' and 'AMH' – representing 'A Barbadian's Head' and 'A Martinican's Head'. Roberts was considered to be the curse of the Caribbean and the flag demonstrates the continuing feud that existed between him and the Governors of the islands of Barbados and Martinique. Another flag that he flew was black with a pirate and a skeleton holding an hourglass between them, signifying that time was running out for his victims. Such was the standing of Bartholomew Roberts that he is also mentioned in Robert Louis Stevenson's *Treasure Island*, first published in 1883. When talking about his amputated leg, Long John Silver states: "That was Roberts' men, that was."

Roberts was not the stereotypical pirate. He had many strict standards, and the large crew he commanded were required to abide by firm written Articles. He did not drink and did not accompany his crew ashore to indulge in extravagant pleasures. It is the supreme irony of Roberts' short but colourful career that it ended when his crew, worse for drink, failed to see the enemy approaching. In

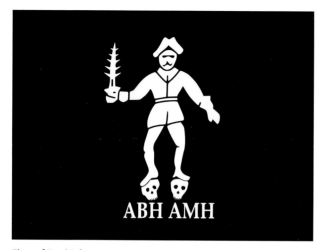

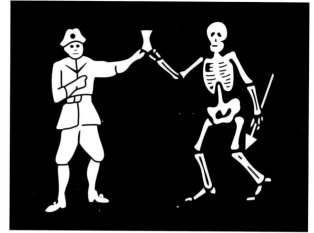

Flags of Barti Ddu

1722, Bartholomew Roberts was killed at the Battle of Cape Lopez when his throat was ripped out by grapeshot from a British Man-of-War, marking the end of the Golden Age of Piracy. His memorial stone can be seen on the village green at Little Newcastle, some 4,000 miles from where he met his end on the coast of Gabon, West Africa. He was quoted as saying, "A merry life and a short one shall be my motto."

In 1844, the quiet village of Little Newcastle once more gained infamy when two of its inhabitants, William (Joseph) Walters and David Vaughan, were convicted at the Pembrokeshire Spring Assizes of Unlawful Assembly and sentenced to a term of twelve months imprisonment. This was for their part in destroying the toll gate at Prendergast, situated at the north entrance to the county town of Haverfordwest. It happened at the height of what became known as the Rebecca Riots. Social unrest and rebellion had first broken out some fifteen miles east in the Preseli Hills five years earlier, in response to the government of the day imposing extortionate levies upon farmers passing along public roads in order to go to market and generally conduct their business.

Though there is no hard evidence to corroborate the claim, it is said that William James, a Welsh Baptist minister also from Little Newcastle, made the decision to emigrate from Pembrokeshire to Pennsylvania. His great-grandson, born in Clay County, Missouri in 1847, was the notorious outlaw Jesse James.

Though Little Newcastle is a small hamlet, this pedigree demonstrates that it is nevertheless significant. It has produced several characters whose notoriety has spread thousands of miles across the globe. Perhaps it was the waters of the River Anghof, once relied upon to baptise worshippers at Beulah Chapel, that inspired a defiant trait in the few.

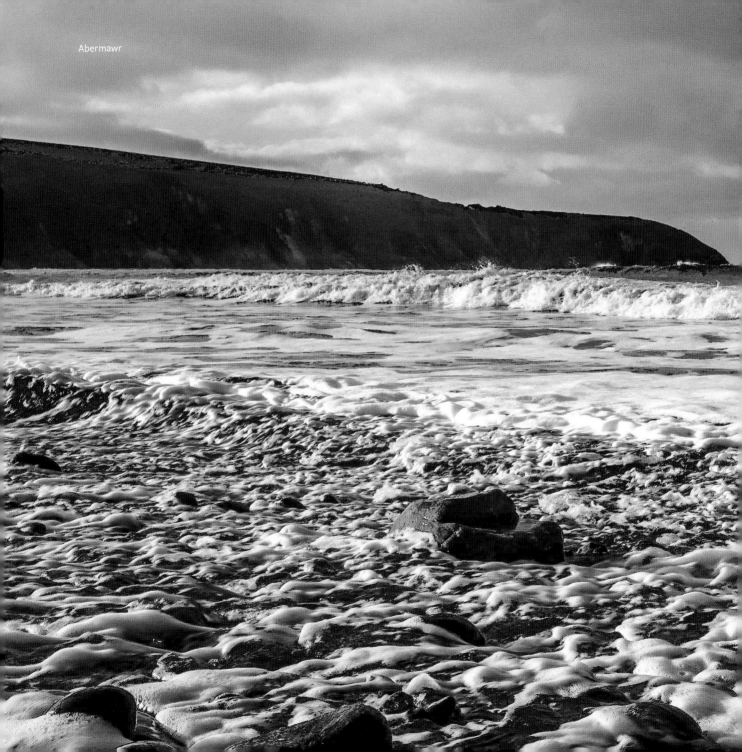

Abermawr

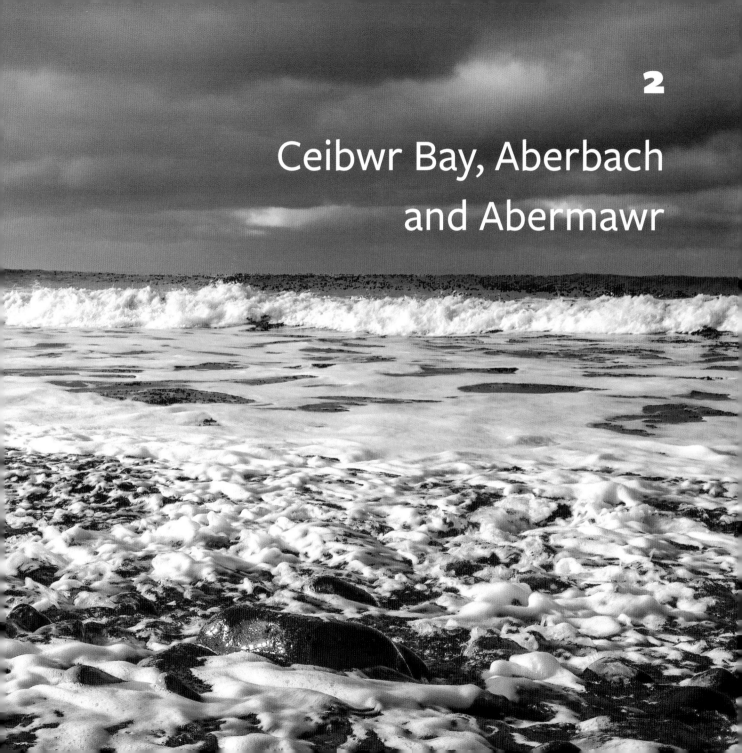

2

Ceibwr Bay, Aberbach and Abermawr

Men of fortune come ashore

THE PRACTICES ASSOCIATED with pirates and smugglers foreran modern-day drug trafficking, which at first blush appears alien to the environment of this county. Such nefarious activities, however, are rooted in history and tend to be replicated time and again. Frequently, the brainpower behind such a profitable criminal enterprise is someone from outside the area who seizes upon an opportunity to remotely manipulate and control the operation, occasionally using a local runner who will have inside knowledge of the region's topography. The isolated nature of the coves and secluded beaches that are common along the coastline north of the Landsker Line means that they have on occasion been deliberately targeted by professional criminal gangs as a safe haven for their trade.

The area north of Newport (Trefdraeth), towards Ceibwr Bay and the steep headland known as Cemaes Head, is the final length of the Pembrokeshire Coast Path, ending at St Dogmaels and the mouth of the Teifi Estuary. Here there is full exposure to the dramatic force of the south-westerly Atlantic, the terrain is rough and the walking can be hard going. Public transport does not accommodate those who wish to explore the lonely, quirky coves to watch over attractive seal pups basking in the months immediately after the summer. The average motorist is daunted by the thought of having to reverse an oversized motor home or a posh car for an oncoming tractor pulling a muck spreader.

The area borders Ceredigion to the north, where the mid 1970s witnessed an invasion by a criminal gang including chemists who manufactured LSD in the vicinity of Tregaron. 'Operation Julie' involved Dyfed-Powys Police with other forces in an undercover police operation and led to arrests and lengthy prison sentences being imposed in 1978.

The area is challenging to any police force, with an expanse of 350 miles of coastline as well as remote rural communities and the activities of hectic tourists to monitor. In 1983 Drug Squad Officers, once more from the Dyfed-Powys force, targeted the rugged coastline south of Ceibwr Bay and Pwll y Wrach when they executed 'Operation Seal Bay'. Through local intelligence they unearthed an underground chamber on Cell-Howel Beach, excavated to stash an estimated three tons of cannabis. Here they also discovered sophisticated radio equipment and other paraphernalia, with a potential to reap millions of pounds for international drug traffickers extending across Europe. Though Interpol and the French police showed a token interest, it was the tenacity and determination of experienced Dyfed-Powys detectives and the curiosity of the people of North Pembrokeshire, rather than international police co-operation, that infiltrated a conspiracy to import controlled drugs via the sea.

The suspicions of local fishermen were aroused and the presence of black plastic sheeting led to the discovery of huge inflatable boats secreted on the beach. On top of this, the extravagant behaviour of strangers in the local pubs of the area, showing off bundles of cash, attracted the notice and curiosity of locals. When the immediate community began to question the spending habits of these outsiders, it led to arrests being made and substantial prison sentences being handed down to eight defendants. Their excesses were no different from the overindulgence of the 'men of fortune' who came ashore in the eighteenth-century Caribbean and took over the local taverns, making themselves equally conspicuous.

Just two years later the picturesque small pebble beach

of Aberbach, north of Abermawr, was targeted by sinister invaders who, as part of a drug-smuggling ring, exploited its isolation. Again, the location was a considered choice, knowing that public access could prove difficult. The average tourist would rather opt for a more straightforward route to a pristine beach with parking and toilet facilities, and maybe an ice-cream van to placate the children. However, once more, Dyfed-Powys Police were not to be outwitted by the interlopers and a further drug smuggling operation was stopped in its tracks.

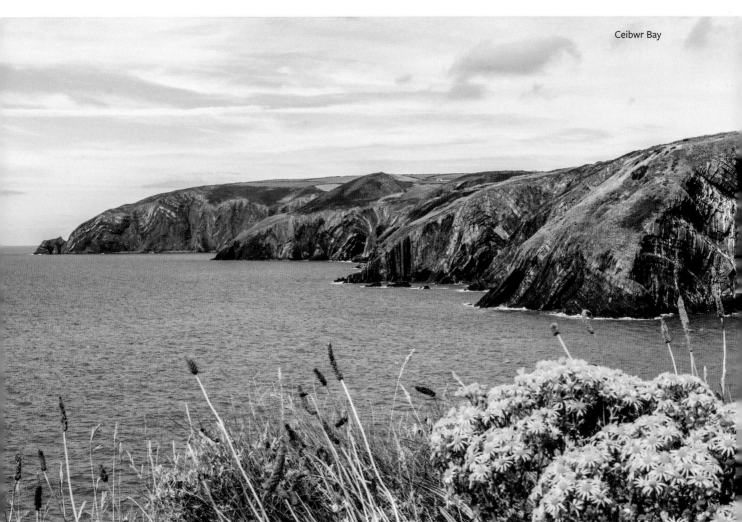

Ceibwr Bay

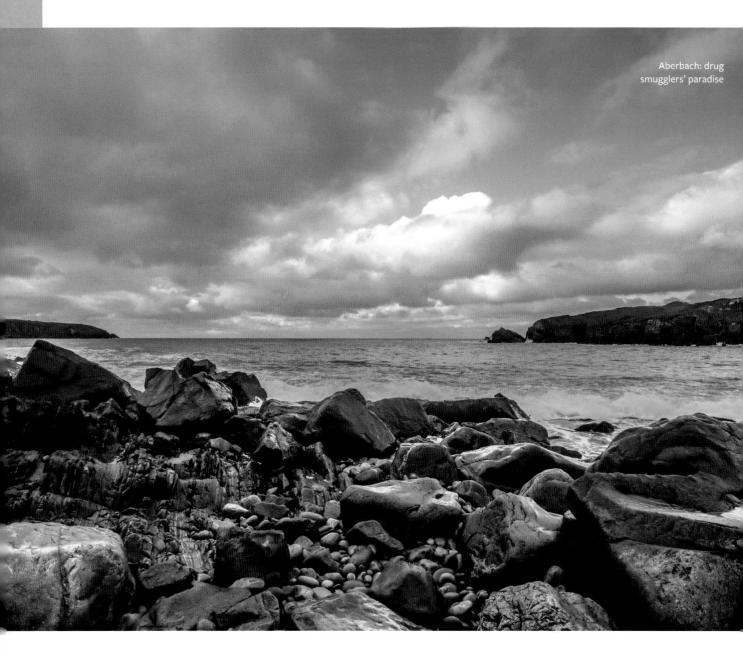

Aberbach: drug
smugglers' paradise

In contrast to recurrent police activity in modern times, the Victorian period heralded a landmark 'invasion' to the west coast of Pembrokeshire through enterprise in engineering and communication. The United Kingdom as a whole was to reap immense benefit.

The Great Western Railway, creating important new links between London, the Midlands and South Wales, was a remarkable feat of engineering, largely due to Isambard Kingdom Brunel. In 1844, a rail link was planned between London Paddington and the Pembrokeshire coast, and eventually to southern Ireland. The western ferry terminal was originally to be located at Abermawr, but the route was changed during the course of construction, and built east of Milford Haven at Neyland.

Communications were further enhanced between 1862 and 1866 with the laying of the Atlantic Cable that would enable telegraph links with Ireland and Newfoundland, Canada. The cable station was built on the Tregwynt Estate at Abermawr, and was vital in providing communication links with North America.

It would be remiss to ignore one further enterprise born during the same period in this isolated and windswept valley on the north coast of Pembrokeshire. What started as a corn mill, part of the same estate at Dyffryn Bach, ultimately became known as Melin Tregwynt. Owned and managed by the Griffiths family for over three generations, it quickly prospered and today prides itself on a worldwide reputation in manufacturing a distinctive brand of Welsh wool fabrics with eye-catching designs.

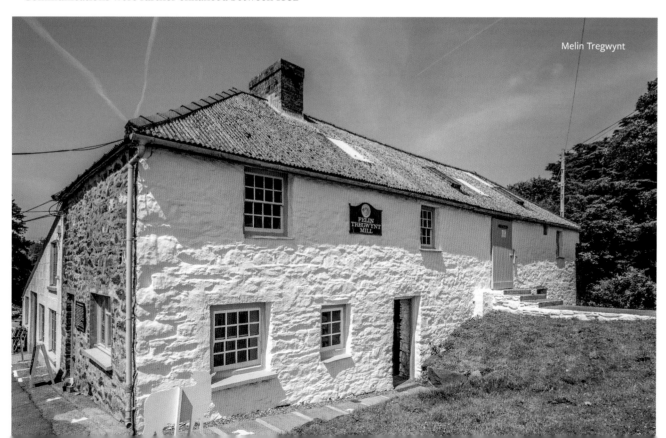

Melin Tregwynt

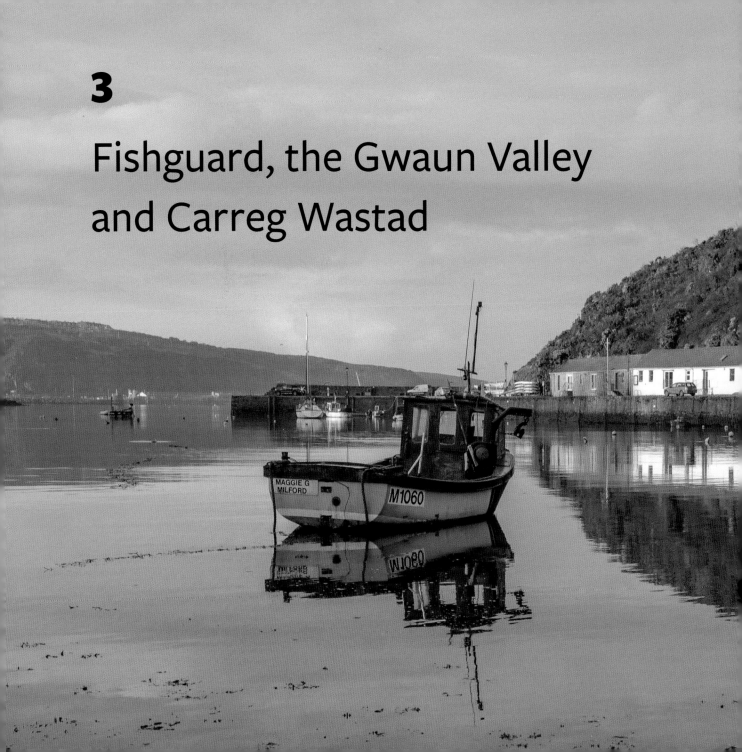

3

Fishguard, the Gwaun Valley and Carreg Wastad

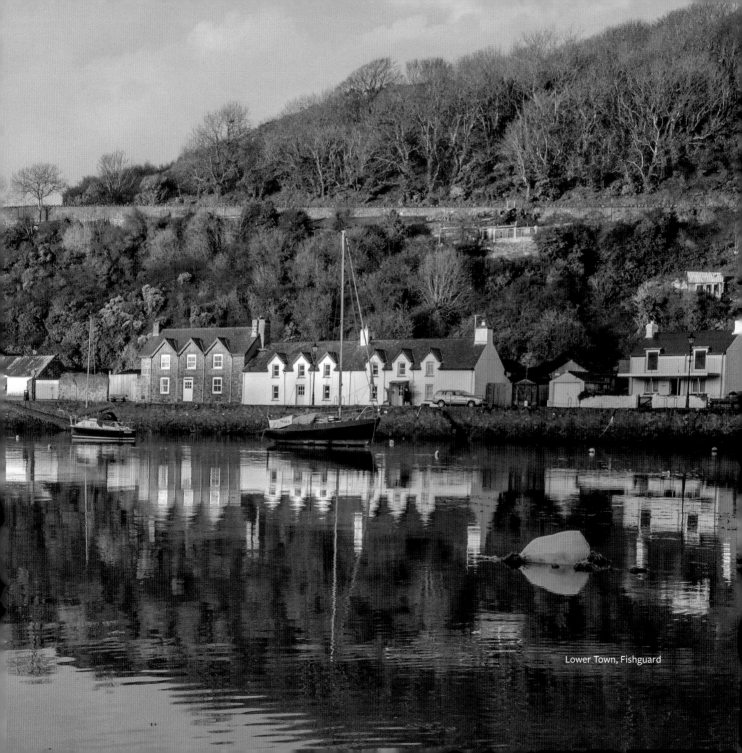

Lower Town, Fishguard

The Julian Calendar and French madness

IN THE LATE tenth century, Vikings invaded the coastline of North Pembrokeshire and commenced trading, choosing to settle in the area. The name Fishguard is derived from the Norse *Fiskigarðr*, meaning 'fish catching enclosure', and had become anglicised by the nineteenth century. The coastline north of Fishguard (Abergwaun) was always recognised as a haunt of salt smugglers. The local fishermen depended upon salt to preserve their catch, and with it being heavily taxed for a long period, they succumbed to illicit means to acquire it.

Fishguard is traditionally a Welsh-speaking community and is divided into two parts. The main town of Fishguard looks down over Goodwick (Wdig) and Lower Town, a community of its own, with views across St George's Channel towards southern Ireland. Lower Town, it is believed, was the original hamlet from which Fishguard developed. It is situated in a deep valley where the River Gwaun meets the sea and ultimately developed as a port, trading with Ireland, Bristol and Liverpool. When directing his film of Dylan Thomas' *Under Milk Wood*, released in 1972, Oxford-born Andrew Sinclair chose the setting of Lower Town for the fictional village of Llareggub. Even with Richard Burton, Elizabeth Taylor, Peter O'Toole and a stellar Welsh cast, the film was not a box-office success, though it is considered a classic today. In 2012, Sinclair graciously gave the rights 'to the people of Wales'.

The 1956 grand adventure film *Moby Dick*, directed by John Huston and starring Gregory Peck as Captain Ahab, was also filmed in Fishguard, with the principal actors stayed at the imposing Fishguard Bay Hotel. Over the years both Huston and Peck spoke about the experience of filming on the perilous Irish Sea and the loss of at least one rubber white whale model, drifting from its moorings into the fog. However, cinematographer Oswald Morris, in his autobiography *Huston, We Have a Problem*, said that the only casualty in the props department was a 20-foot-high cylinder representing the middle section of the 'lost whale', which broke from its tow line and floated away.

Back in the eighteenth century, however, Lower Town was of interest to seafarers and villagers of a different kind to such characters as Dylan's Captain Cat, Rosie Probert and Polly Garter. In 1779, when Britain was actively engaged 3,000 miles away in trying to suppress the American colonists in their War of Independence (1775–1782), the area was targeted by an invader who had been commissioned to further the revolutionary cause. Stephen Manhant, who originated from Boston, USA, captained the *Black Prince*, a privateer vessel sailing under a French flag. He issued a ransom demand of £1,000 to the town, and when the people of Fishguard refused to pay, a salvo of cannon shot was fired on some houses, also damaging St Mary's Church. Thereafter a fortress was built, which was later used to defend the area from potential invaders during the Napoleonic Wars.

In the immediate locality – but away from the coast and commercial razzmatazz – is the mysterious Gwaun Valley, sought out by the more discerning tourist for its beauty, and where inhabitants celebrate *Hen Galan* (the old New Year) according to the Julian calendar, on 13 January.

Though in 1752 Great Britain and its colonies followed the practice of many countries and replaced the Julian calendar with the Gregorian calendar, named after Pope Gregory XIII, the people of the Gwaun Valley resisted the change, perhaps fearing a return to Catholicism.

To this day, the tradition known as *Calennig* continues, with children singing "*Blwyddyn Newydd dda i chi*" and being given sweets or money in return. Also embraced is the ritual of the Mari Llwyd, where a horse's skull – often a wooden reproduction – is paraded on a pole decorated with ribbons and greenery to bring good luck and fortune to the houses visited.

The inquisitive visitor will often wander off the well-known trail here, in search of one of the county's typical one-pub villages. There are some inimitable characters, with one in particular standing out: Bessie Davies – 'Aunty Bessie' – of the Dyffryn Arms, Pontfaen has been pouring traditional ales from the jug and helping wayfarers from all around the world for over 66 years.

The public house was originally a family home before its conversion to licensed premises. 'Bessie's' has been in the family since 1840 and is one of the few surviving rural pubs of late Georgian design. The melodious tone of a West Midlands accent can often be heard in the quiet bar of her home, which is pure nostalgia, unadulterated by digitised menus and service tills.

Pwllderi and Strumble Head provide an outstanding

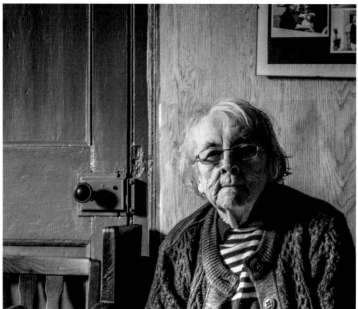

'Aunty Bessie', Pontfaen, Cwm Gwaun

panoramic outlook southwards towards St Davids Head. Here there is an air of complete tranquillity that doubtless gave inspiration to Dewi Emrys (1881–1952), winner of the Crown at the National Eisteddfod in 1926 and the Chair on four occasions between 1929 and 1948, to write '*Pwllderi*'. This poem was written in the Welsh dialect of northern Pembrokeshire.

Though he is buried in Talgarreg, Ceredigion, a couplet from the work is inscribed on his memorial stone at Pwllderi:

A THINA'R MEDDILIE SY'N DWAD ICHI
PAN FOCH CHI'N ISHTE UWCHBEN PWLLDERI
(And these are the thoughts that come to you
When you sit above Pwllderi)

Towards the end of the eighteenth century, however, that peacefulness was seriously disturbed when a French invasion from the sea landed just north-east of this location. The area witnessed a ragtag crew who were not there for the scenery, and who went on the rampage.

On 22 February 1797 four French ships carrying 1,400

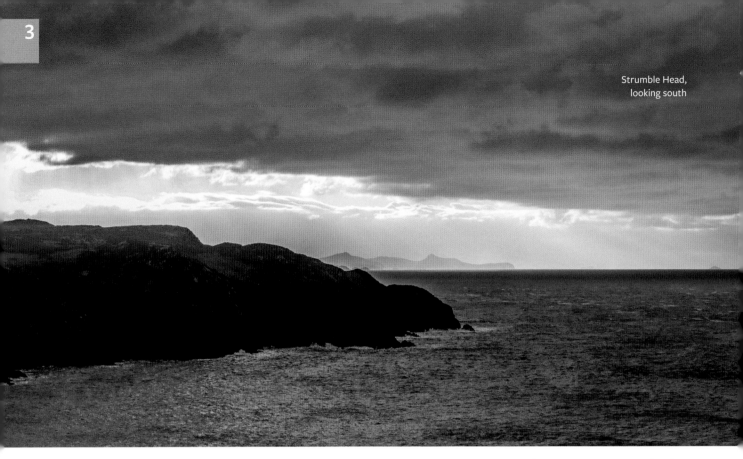

Strumble Head,
looking south

troops – including several hundred conscripted, many of whom were deserters or convicts – under the command of Irish-American Colonel Tate, were part of a failed military invasion of mainland Britain that landed at Carreg Wastad, an isolated inlet on the Llanwnda Peninsula only accessible from the Coastal Path or from the sea. The story behind this foray is that whilst Napoleon Bonaparte was making territorial strides across Italy, revolutionary France was seeking to muster support from Ireland and its Celtic neighbours to initiate an uprising against the English.

Having landed about two miles south of Fishguard and taken possession of Trehowel Farm, many ran riot, looting isolated smallholdings, before surrendering two days later on Goodwick Sands to the local militia force led by Lord Cawdor, and were promptly incarcerated in Haverfordwest Castle. The eccentric behaviour of the invaders and how they came to lay down their arms has been the subject of incessant speculation over the years. One popular theory is that the invading force, in a drunken haze, thought that local Welsh women, traditionally dressed in tall black hats and red cloaks, were British soldiers. Figuring prominently in the apprehension of the invaders was Jemima Nicholas. Urban myth or fact has elevated her into a daunting character, a Welsh heroine who 'single-handedly' captured

12 soldiers with pitchfork in hand. She reportedly then locked them up in St Mary's Church, in whose churchyard she is now buried.

Fishguard is today an important ferry terminal providing a link between Ireland and mainland Britain, though it has just two daily Irish crossings to Rosslare. On 28 August 2019, however, the sleepy port was rocked when one of the largest hauls of cocaine in UK history was found on board a boat, the *SY Atrevido*, which had sailed from South America into waters about half a mile off the Welsh coast. *Atrevido* in Spanish means 'daring' or 'cheeky', and this was indeed a daring criminal enterprise, but one which was swiftly detected. The boat was targeted as part of an intelligence-led operation by the National Crime Agency and the Border Force with the assistance of the Spanish police, and was intercepted before reaching its intended destination and escorted into Fishguard harbour. The operation led to the arrest of two British nationals from Liverpool, and the seizure of 750 kg of the Class A drug, worth an estimated £60 million.

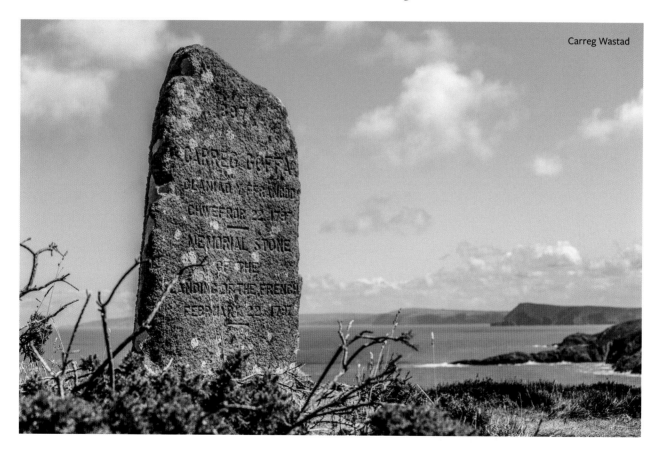

Carreg Wastad

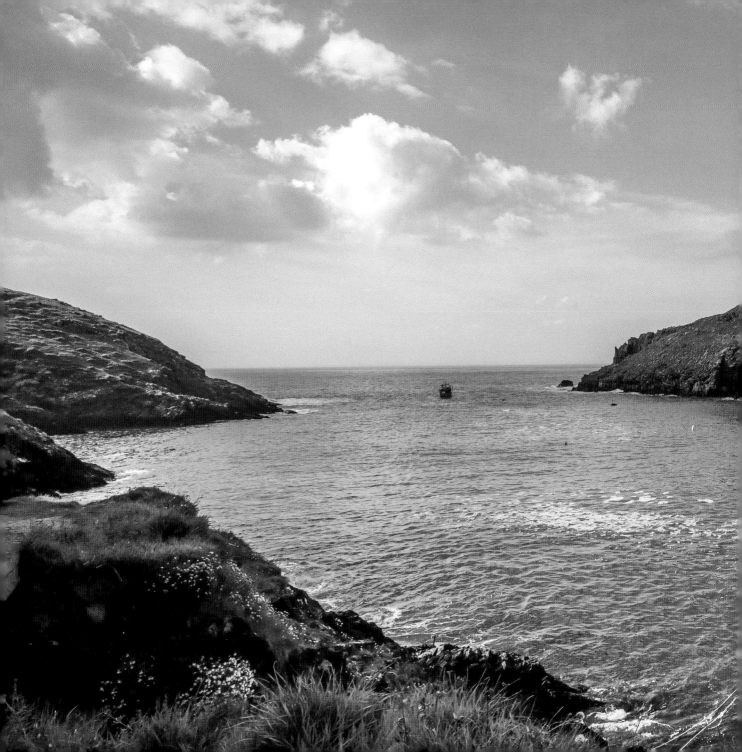

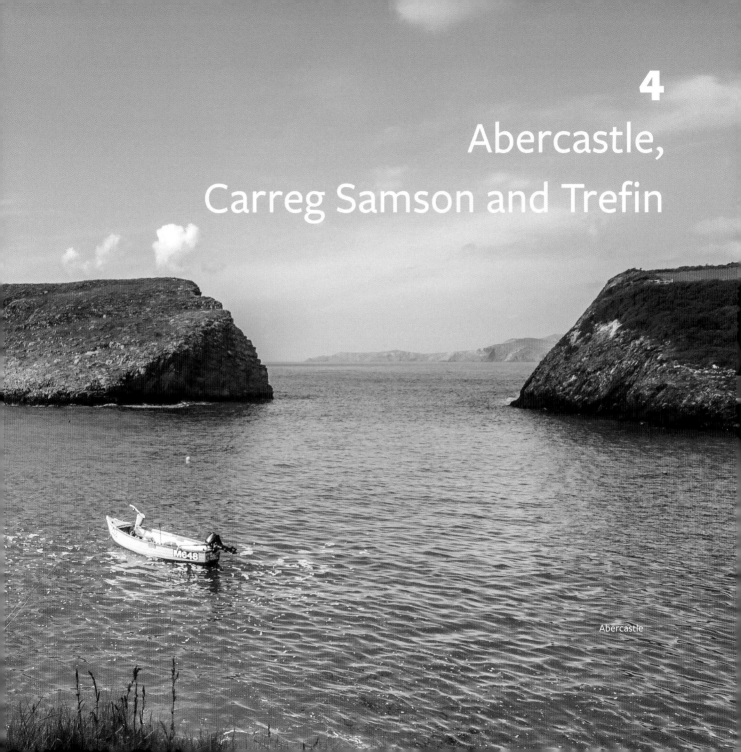

4

Abercastle,
Carreg Samson and Trefin

Abercastle

An American gamble and a literary link

ALMOST 80 YEARS after the French debacle at Carreg Wastad, a few miles further south saw the landing of a lone sailor who had made the solo crossing of the Atlantic from Gloucester, Massachusetts to Abercastle. He was bound for Liverpool but was forced to take refuge some distance short. It may be that the twenty-first century cocaine gang had planned a similar route before getting cut off at Fishguard.

On 12 August 1876 Alfred Johnson, a Danish-born fisherman, successfully made the unprecedented voyage, contrary to the expectations of some friends. He claimed to be the first recorded person to make the single handed crossing 3,000 miles from west to east. Having set out on 15 June 1876, this incredible feat was achieved in sixty-six days to mark the centenary of the birth of the

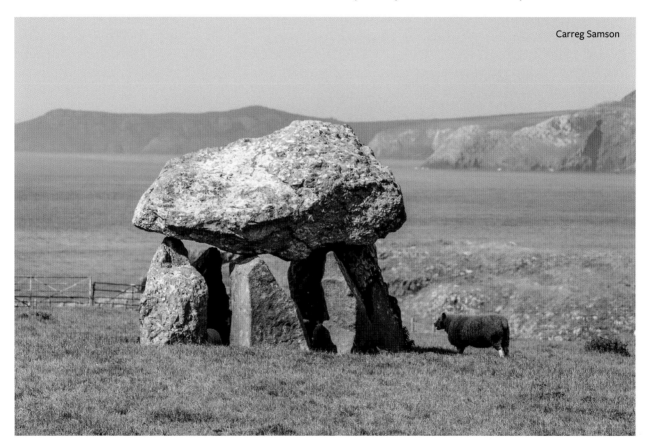

Carreg Samson

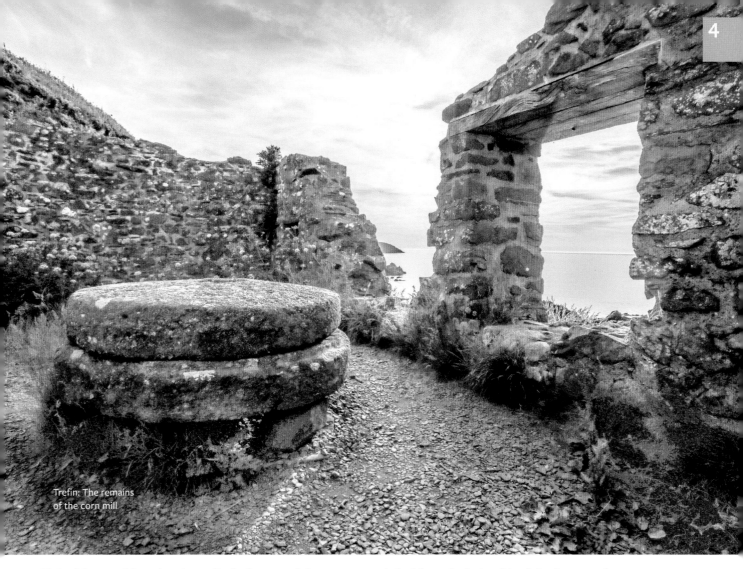

Trefin: The remains of the corn mill

United States of America. Accordingly, he named the 20-foot fishing dory that carried him *Centennial*. His Viking ancestors would doubtless have been impressed by his navigational skills but probably at a loss to understand his motive in undertaking such a reckless venture, with little return apart from the kudos earned from a dare made by his card-playing friends back across the water.

Overlooking the bay where lonely mariner Alfred Johnson first set foot on the beach at Abercastle (Abercastell) is the imposing sight of the Neolithic burial chamber known as Carreg Samson. This magnificent megalithic tomb was of great significance when erected

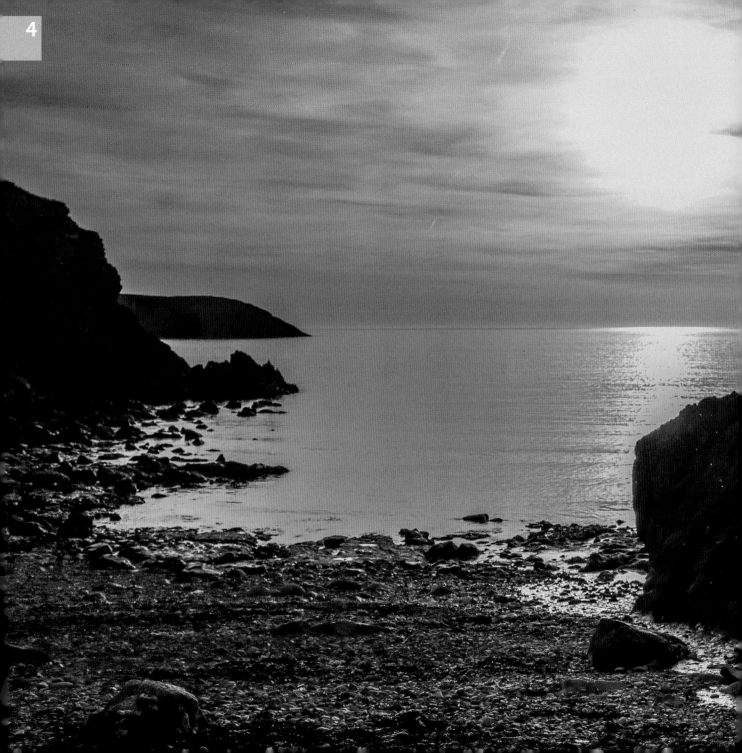

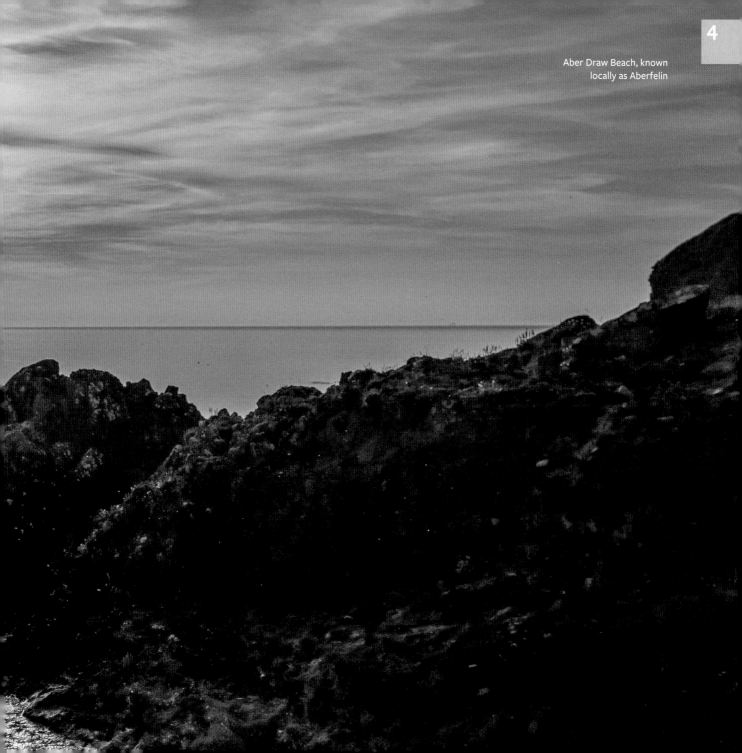

Aber Draw Beach, known
locally as Aberfelin

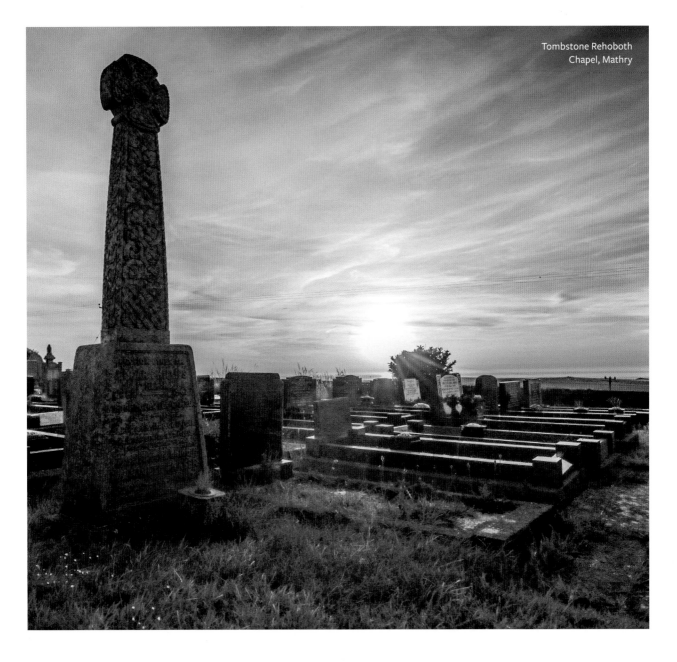

Tombstone Rehoboth
Chapel, Mathry

by folk who arrived by sea some 6,000 years before his intrepid crossing. The story goes that St Samson of Dol lifted the large capstone, measuring some 15 ft by 9 ft, onto three of the six upright stones with his little finger, something we may find even more implausible than the wager made by Johnson's betting friends.

The small village of Trefin, flanked by Aber Draw (Aberfelin) Beach, bears witness to the remains of one of many corn mills that were once common throughout the county. Melin Trefin served the agricultural community for over 500 years. Wheat was milled into flour for bread, and barley was ground to make winter fodder for farm animals. The stream running alongside once powered its former water wheel. By 1900 it was already in decline, possibly due to the repeal of the Corn Laws in 1846 and the relaxation of import duties. Cheap grain imported from overseas and mass production in the large industrial towns, together with the reduced cost of shipping, saw its closure in 1918.

This foreshadowed the recurrent theme of a community having to struggle with a depressed economy caused by the importing of cheap commodities as a means of achieving free trade in agriculture. The consequence would invariably see a decline in local skills and employment.

Trefin can also lay claim to two particularly noteworthy literary links. Firstly, William Williams (1875–1968), who is largely remembered as poet 'Crwys' and served as Archdruid at the National Eisteddfod of Wales between 1939 and 1947. He was the author of 'Melin Trefin', an allegorical poem drawing parallels between the life of the mill and the short lifetime of the miller, using alliteration, rhythm and rhyme. The last verse is perhaps particularly poignant:

Segur faen sy'n gwylio fangre
Yn y curlaw mawr a'r gwynt,
Di-lythyren garreg goffa
O'r amseroedd difyr gynt,
Ond does yma neb yn malu,
Namyn amser swrth a'r hin
Wrthi'n chwalu ac yn malu,
Malu'r felin yn Nhrefin.

(The stone at rest that watches the place
in the thrashing rain and the wind
is a letterless memorial
to the jollity of former times.
Nobody is milling here now.
It is a time of dereliction
the grinding down
of the mill at Trefin.

– Translation by Sharon Larkin)

Secondly, Edgar Phillips (1889–1962) took his bardic name, 'Trefin', from his birthplace and served as Archdruid from 1960 until his death. His memorial is at Rehoboth Chapel, a few miles away, with an undisturbed vista overlooking Abercastle.

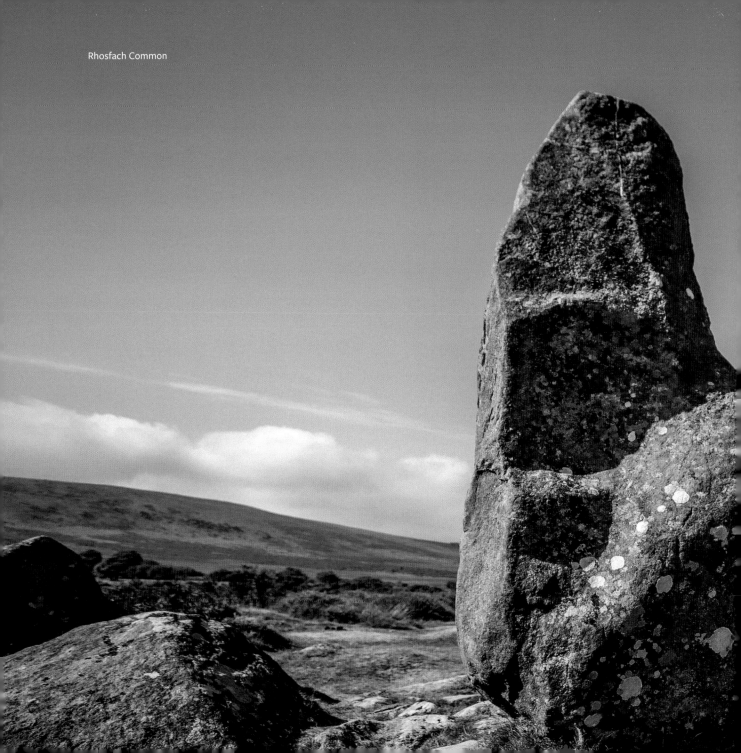

5
Preseli, Mynachlog-Ddu and Efailwen

Secular and religious nonconformity

THE PRESELI HILLS, just over ten miles north of Narberth, mostly lie within the Pembrokeshire National Park. This attractive but remote range, known as *Mynyddoedd y Preselau* in Welsh, crosses the spine of the county and reaches its peak of 1,759 ft at Foel Cwmcerwyn. It is an area of outstanding natural beauty that is not entirely without controversy, and has witnessed episodes of historical dissension.

One issue that has perplexed both geologists and archaeologists and sparked years of intense academic debate is the issue of the 'movement' of spotted blue dolerite stone during the Neolithic period, 4,000 to 5,000 years ago, from the Preseli Hills to Salisbury Plain, 160 miles away to the east. What accounts for the presence of these stones, which form the smaller upright Inner Circle of bluestones at Stonehenge? Was the rock transported to the area as a result of glacial movement up the Bristol Channel, or was it achieved through the human haulage of 80 monoliths, each weighing many tons, from the area of Brynberian and Rhosfach Common across difficult terrain, over the Welsh border into Wiltshire? A recent study of debris through radiocarbon dating in craggy outcrops of rock at Carn Goedog and Craig Rhos-y Felin suggests human movement as opposed to geological forces.

It is a fact that there are a number of Neolithic dolmen or portal tombs – burial chambers – within the county that must have required immense human physical strength to erect. In the immediate vicinity of Brynberian, for instance, stands the largest of the megalithic burial chambers – Pentre Ifan, dating back to 3500 BC. The elegant capstone, weighing over 16 tons, rests upon three upright stones, some 8 ft off the ground. The argument that getting the stone to Stonehenge was achieved through sheer physical human strength and determination, rather than geological movement, still remains a contentious issue today.

These inspiring hills have been the scene of conflict on the occasions when the government of the day has sought to subjugate and attack the secular and religious rights of those living and farming the land in and around Preseli. Those whose rights were being compromised can be seen as victims of trespass and flagrant acts of piracy in the name of the Crown. The most recent occasion was in 1947, when the War Office put forward a proposal to confiscate in excess of 16,000 acres of land in the north of the county and to evict over 200 farmers from their homes and land. The rationale behind this outrageous plan was that the area was to be used as a permanent training ground for the British Army. Fortunately, that scheme was successfully resisted by a determined and collaborative effort on the part of the community, commemorated in Hefin Wyn's book, *Battle of the Preselau 1946–1948*.

R Parri Roberts, minister at Bethel Baptist Chapel, Mynachlog-Ddu, and many other distinguished Nonconformist ministers and local headmasters figured prominently in the campaign, determined to safeguard the Preseli Hills from seizure. When confronted by military officers, 'Parri Bach' fittingly described the spirit of the Preseli inhabitants in the phrase: "We nurture souls in this area." Waldo Williams (1904–1971), virtuous pacifist and poet brought up in Mynachlog-ddu, gained his inspiration at Bwlch Gwynt and composed 'Preseli', which appeared on the front page of the Welsh-language national weekly paper *Y Faner,* and described the War Office as "*y bwystfil*" (the beast). The fight put up by

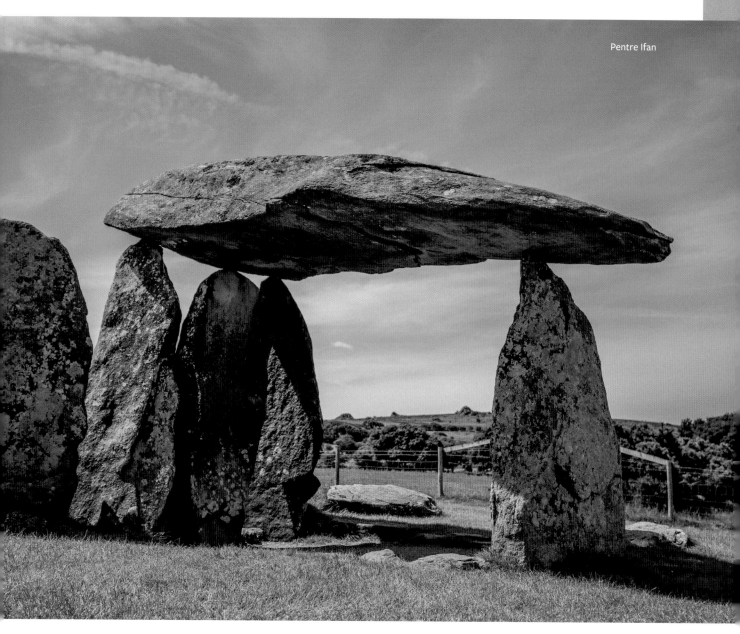

Pentre Ifan

locals made it possible for hill walkers today to gain solitude and pleasure from rambling over these 'sacred hills', untainted by military presence.

Though this region is very much inland, cultural and linguistic diversity exists – coinciding once more with the Landsker partition. Place names alert the tourist to significant differences. For instance, travelling north from Woodstock (Wstog) in the parish of Ambleston (Treamlod), through Glynsaethmaen and arriving at Efailwen, the linguistic and cultural divide is apparent. This is the area where the counties of Pembrokeshire and Carmarthenshire almost touch each other.

In days gone by, the once monoglot Welsh-speaking communities of Llanfallteg (which was in Pembrokeshire prior to the straightening of the county boundary in 1974), Llangolman and Llanglydwen were no strangers to social strife and rebellion against an oppressive and unsympathetic English government, once more intent on violating the rights of people trying to cope with social and economic deprivation. In the early nineteenth century the agricultural community of Efailwen, along with other areas of south and mid Wales were targeted by the turnpike trusts, created by Acts of Parliament to maintain the roads. However, they were soon seen as a levy on poverty-stricken farmers as tollgates were erected along the highways habitually used by agricultural workers, who were required to pay a charge in order to proceed. To add insult to injury, those responsible for extorting the tax often charged extortionate rates and dishonestly diverted the monies elsewhere.

The evening of 13 May 1839 saw the first demonstration of social unrest with the first destruction in Wales of a tollgate, which had been erected at Efailwen. Farmers passing through on a regular basis with their livestock to market at Narberth (Arberth) were saddled with an unduly onerous financial burden. Thomas Rees (Twm Carnabwth, 1806–1876) is credited as being the leader of the first episode of what became known as the Rebecca Riots (*Merched Beca*, 1839–1843), in which gangs of local agricultural workers, often dressed as women to disguise their identities, attacked and destroyed tollgates and tollhouses around west and mid Wales. Rees lived at Glynsaethmaen, where apparently this conspiracy to end the toll-road iniquity was hatched. He regularly worshipped at the Nonconformist Bethel Chapel, Mynachlog-ddu, where he was at the forefront of the Welsh *pwnc* (*Cymanfa Bwnc*), a form of religious chanting from the Bible, and it is here that he is buried. Over 100 years later, R Parri Roberts preached from the same pulpit. The gravestones of both, for some reason, contain incorrect inscriptions as to their respective dates of birth.

Twm's tombstone bears the inscription:

Er cof am THOMAS REES trial o'r plwyf hwn
bu marw Med 17 1876 yn 70 oed Twm Carnabwth
Nid oes neb ond Duw yn gwybod
Beth a ddigwydd mewn diwrnod.
Wrth gyrchu bresych at fy nginio,
Daeth angau i fy ngardd i'm taro
(No one but God knows what may happen in one day.
While fetching a cabbage for my dinner,
death came into my garden and struck me)

Religious justification for the actions of Rebecca and her daughters was said to be found in the Bible in a passage from Genesis 24:60: 'And they blessed Rebekah, and said unto her… Let thy seed possess the gate of those which hate them.'

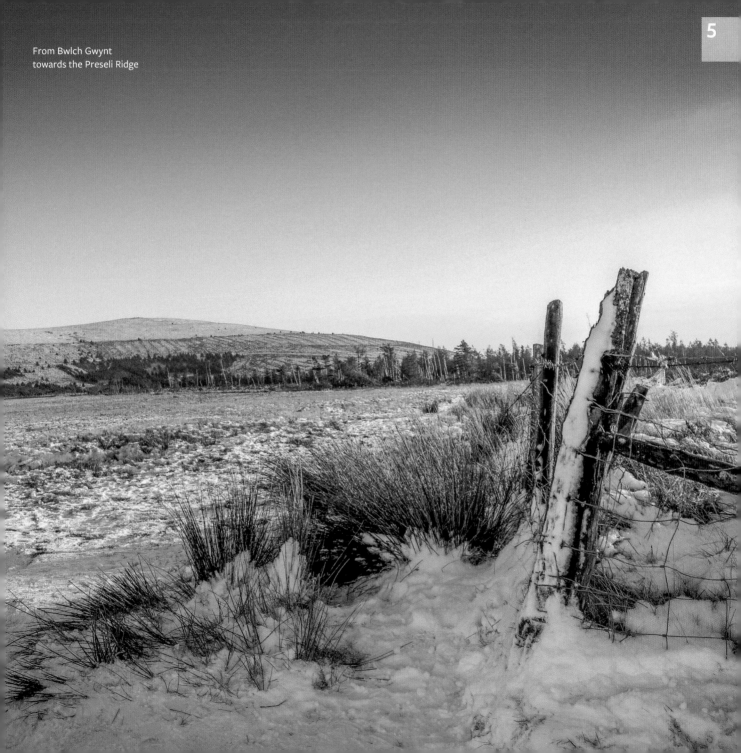

From Bwlch Gwynt
towards the Preseli Ridge

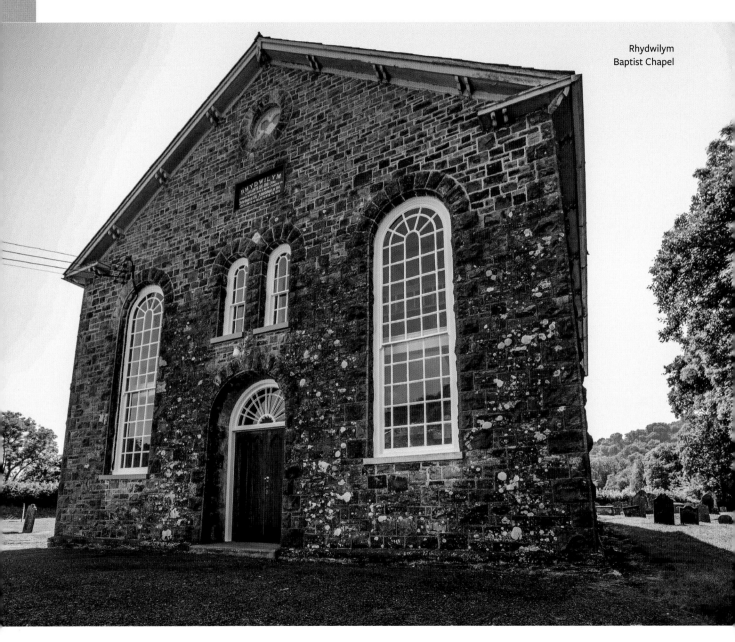

Rhydwilym
Baptist Chapel

In 1992, the film *Rebecca's Daughters*, the screenplay of which had been written by Dylan Thomas in 1948 and which was directed by Karl Francis, was released. The cast included Peter O'Toole, Dafydd Hywel, the late Ray Gravell and Joely Richardson. It is a great tribute to the legendary Welsh International, British Lion and Llanelli RFC centre that O'Toole stood in awe of Grav – 'Ray o'r Mynydd' (his bardic name), the Grand Sword Bearer at the National Eisteddfod. It was set in South Wales and captured the issue of the oppressive gentry classes of the time, alongside the feisty resistance of the agricultural workers dressed as 'Rebecca' who stormed the tollgates that prevented their passing.

Another form of summary justice that can be associated with social unrest amongst the labouring classes and was common throughout west Wales at this time was known as the *Ceffyl Pren* (Wooden Horse). This took the form of punishing wrongdoers, such as informants and those who had behaved badly in a community, through revealing their wrongdoing and publicly humiliating them by carrying them on a wooden frame through their village. Like Rebecca and her daughters, the jury would blacken their faces and wear women's clothing as a disguise.

The significant and fervent connection between secular and religious nonconformity in the isolated hills of Preseli was reflected across the country. John Davies, in his scholarly masterpiece *A History of Wales*, held the view that 'the chapel people were the only true Welsh and that Welshness was synonymous with Nonconformity'.

Attempts were made to standardise religious practice from Westminster when in 1662 the Act of Uniformity required all churchmen across England and Wales to use only the rites and ceremonies of the Established Church of England, as prescribed in the Book of Common Prayer. Those who did not conform were ejected and discriminated against, being excluded from holding public office or obtaining university degrees from the two ancient universities of Oxford and Cambridge. Some 2,000 in all were ejected from the Church (The Great Ejection).

The Baptist movement in Pembrokeshire was started at Rushacre and Molleston, near Narberth, in 1668 by William Jones, who had been imprisoned for his Nonconformity and served a sentence of four years imprisonment at Carmarthen Castle after the Act of Uniformity. The congregation then moved to the Baptist Chapel at Rhydwilym when it was built in 1701. This is the oldest Baptist church in west Wales and stands in Llandissilio East. It ranks as the mother church of all Baptist Chapels in Pembrokeshire, western Carmarthenshire and southern Ceredigion.

The Landsker division also demarcates a schism in religious worship. The north was a strong breeding ground of Nonconformity, whilst to the south Catholicism and Anglicanism prospered.

A further source of social discontent that served to underline this division was the imposition of Church Tithes. The Anglican Church would appropriate one tenth of the annual income of the labouring classes. Initially it took the form of payment in kind such as crops, wool, milk and other produce, but with the passing of the Tithe Commutation Act in 1836, cash payment was demanded. This even applied to Nonconformist farmers who had no affiliation to the Church, and sparked protest and confrontation, which ultimately led to the burden of payment being placed upon the landlord rather than the tenant farmer.

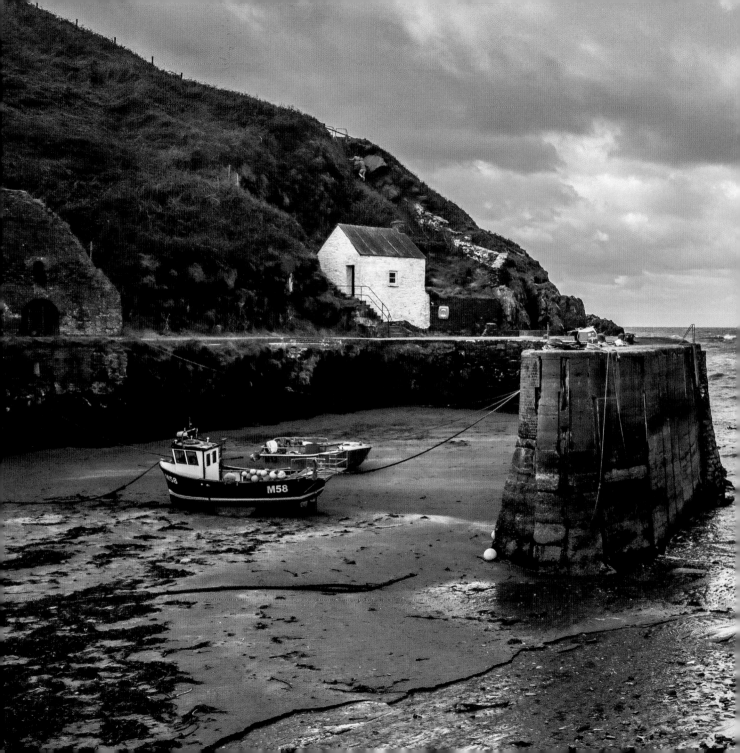

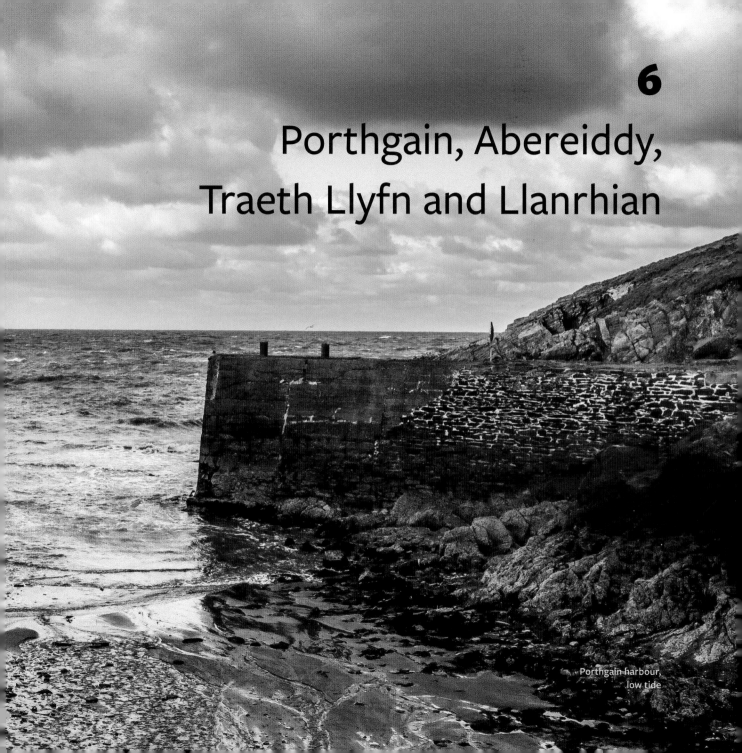

6

Porthgain, Abereiddy, Traeth Llyfn and Llanrhian

Porthgain harbour,
low tide

An industrial paradise

PORTHGAIN AND ABEREIDDY (Abereiddi) are located in the community of Llanrhian, on the coast north of St Davids. Both inlets hide an industrial past easily forgotten, though the remains are still visible when the discerning eye is diverted from the striking scenery that prevails here.

In the nineteenth century, Porthgain was transformed from a small fishing village into an industrial hub and then in 1931 was abruptly shut down overnight, before fishing resumed and tourism later thrived. Though Porthgain has long been associated with slate production, it was quarried either side of the village long before the harbour was constructed. To the west, quarrying occurred at what is now known as the 'Blue Lagoon' in Abereiddy as early as 1838. A much older source was found at Trwyn Llwyd to the east. In the early years all three quarries were operated by a London-based syndicate. The slate industry dominated both Porthgain and Abereiddy between 1850 and 1910.

By 1851, the Crown Estates Commissioners released land in order that a small, deep and naturally sheltered harbour could be built at Porthgain. It was created specifically to export slate. The slate from Abereiddy was conveyed two miles by horse-drawn tramway to Porthgain and then exported from what grew into a thriving harbour. Tramways were also laid through underground tunnels for the same purpose. The quarry workers occupied a small group of houses known as 'The Street' (Y *Stryd*). In 1910, the quarry at Abereiddy was abandoned and flooded by the sea.

A series of companies reinvigorated the industry by investing in new machinery and re-laying the tramway as a narrow-gauge railway track, but were unable to stave off bankruptcy. Many a consortium over the years embarked upon business in the three quarries, only to be later forceed into liquidation. The decline of the slate industry saw the emergence of a new enterprise in 1889: brickmaking, which continued until 1912. It is estimated that 50,000 bricks per week were made in a brickmaking shed known as Tŷ Mawr. The large stone building, facing the harbour, is today a successful seafood restaurant. The tall chimney, once an integral part of that industry, has been demolished.

Another commercial venture initiated alongside brickmaking was the quarrying of granite at Penclegyr. This was crushed into gravel chippings to lay roads. However, due to a number of external factors including worldwide economic depression, the road-stone era came to an unexpected end in 1931. The demise of industrial activity at Porthgain had the consequence of also ending the regular arrival of ships into the harbour waiting to export quarried materials. The business side of the industry was simply abandoned overnight, with papers and accounting records left open in a deserted office. Quarry locomotives stood idle in the engine shop and the trucks associated with transportation of materials were left isolated at the side of the harbour.

Today, derelict brick buildings are to be seen, and the old weighbridge remains visible. The tramways are overgrown, but remain as a testament to what was once a prosperous working passage between Abereiddy and Porthgain – today, a popular scenic walk. It is perhaps ironic that the final scene of the closure of an era of industry occurred with a freak event in 1932, when the whole terrace once occupied by the workers of Abereiddy was washed away by a great storm.

In the 1980s, more than half a century after the end of

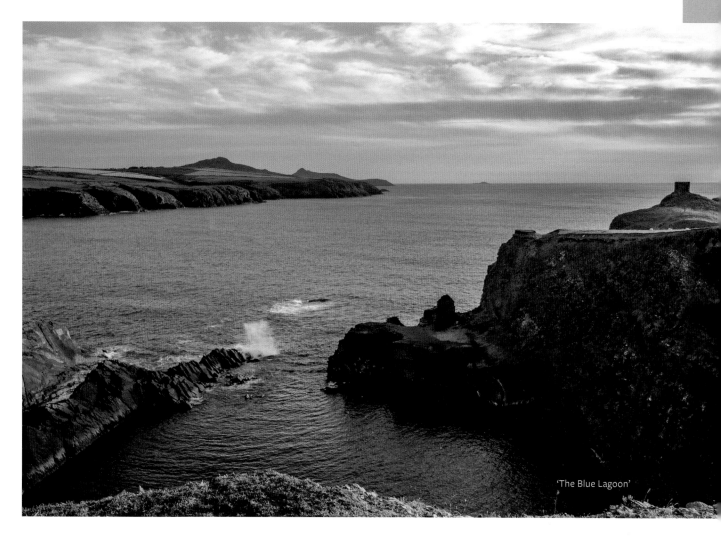

'The Blue Lagoon'

heavy industry there, the village was again threatened. The company GR-Stein Refractories Ltd, previously a brick-manufacturing company based in Sheffield and the former owners of Porthgain and the land around the harbour, were proposing a new development which could have commercialised the village beyond recognition and jeopardised the homes of tenants who had been living there for a lifetime. Fortunately, any notion of corporate

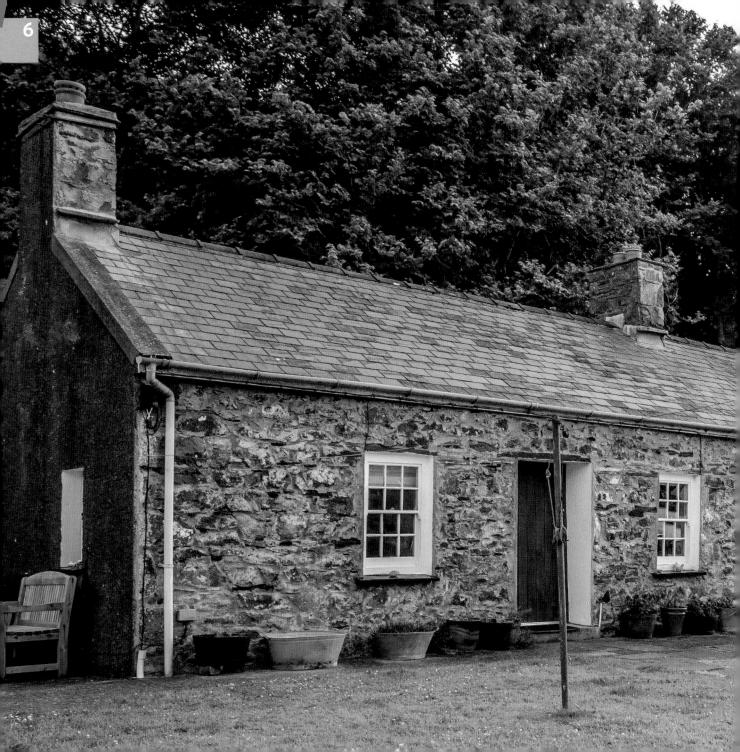

Homes of Porthgain residents

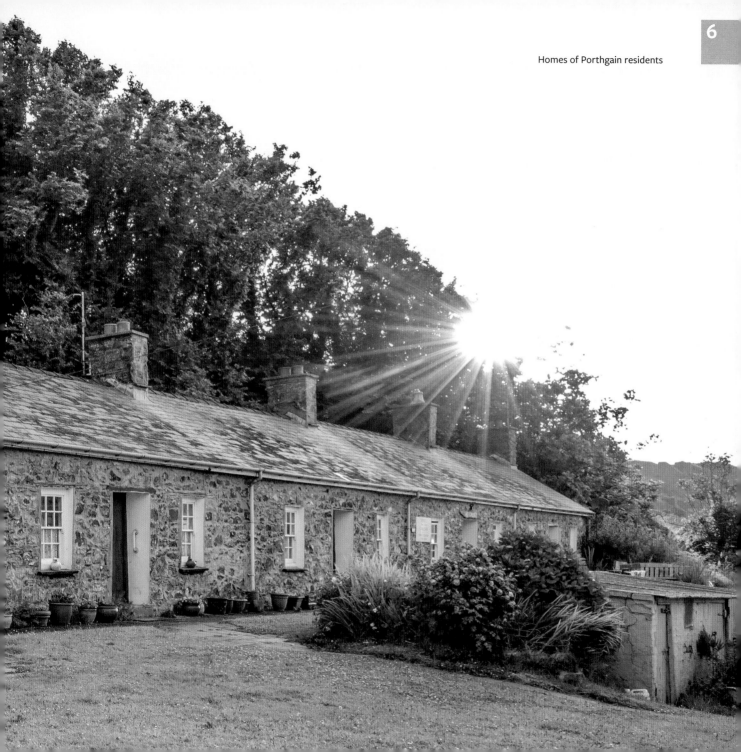

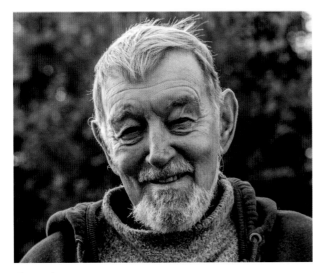

Alun Davies

development was cut short when an agreement was reached that enabled local residents to buy their own homes and retain the village's identity, with the National Park Authority purchasing land around the harbour and the centre of the village. Local artist Alun Davies was instrumental in resolving this worrying issue in favour of the community of Porthgain.

The whole face of Porthgain has been transformed into a playground for tourists, with the emergence of quality eating places where fish is locally sourced leading to a parallel resurgence in fishing. It is also very much a destination for visiting industrial archaeologists.

Equidistant between Porthgain and Abereiddy is a hidden gem: Traeth Llyfn Beach. Considerable credit should be given to Italian prisoners of war working on the surrounding farms immediately after World War II, who apparently also cut in and built the steep steps that lead to the secluded shore and what many consider is

sheer paradise. Their painstaking toil has relieved many a family of what would otherwise be a difficult climb to the top. High above, there are outstanding views out to sea, in particular towards St David's Head, Carn Penberry and Carn Llidi.

The waters along this stretch of the coast were particularly treacherous to shipping. The two navigation beacons at the entrance to Porthgain harbour and the watchtower on the headland of Trwyncastell above Abereiddy bear witness to this. Valuable wreckage could be salvaged here, out of sight of the authorities, and the surrounding coves were once the haunt of smugglers. In Cornwall, it was the practice of wreckers to lure ships onto rocks by placing lighted beacons at strategic points. The 1961 film *Fury at Smugglers' Bay*, starring Peter Cushing, seeks to depict the activities of smugglers in the south-west of England, but was actually shot around Abereiddy. In 2017, Bill Nighy and Gemma Arterton were also on location in Porthgain and Freshwater West to film the 1940s-set comedy-drama, *Their Finest*.

In 2014 the community of Llanrhian saw an intruder of a very different kind, who had sinister and deceitful motives. Local vegetable farmer and agricultural engineer Robert Rees, renowned for his annual crop of *tato newi* (new potatoes), was bewildered when he received a penalty notice alleging that he had parked his vehicle, registration number GDE 167, illegally in Abbey Road, London. The mystery further deepened when another penalty notice arrived at his homestead Pant Bach, accompanied by a photograph showing a Vauxhall Astra bearing the same licence plate and claiming that the vehicle had been involved in a moving traffic offence in Central London.

Rob Rees had never taken a vehicle to London. He had only ever taken the train to Paddington when visiting.

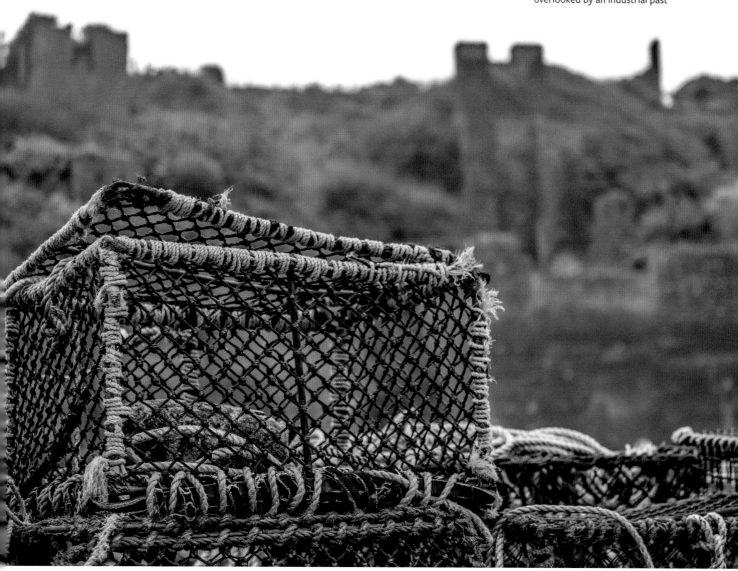

Porthgain: Lobster pots
overlooked by an industrial past

Porthgain | Abereiddy | Traeth Llyfn | Llanrhian

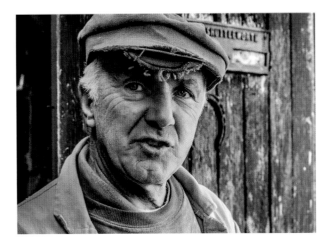

Robert Rees, Llanrhian

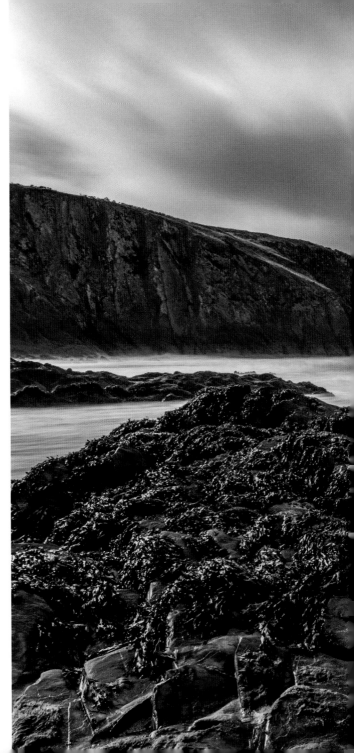

The registration number mentioned in the summons is assigned to a 1945 Oliver Standard 80, one of 30 vintage tractors owned by colourful character Rees. The tractor had not in fact left Pembrokeshire, but an unknown fraudster had cloned the registration to be used for nefarious reasons 260 miles away.

Inevitably, there have been fundamental changes to the fabric of the whole county, its character and its people. This particular corner, though, has witnessed a great depth of change through constant invasion in one form or another. In physical terms it is essentially much as it ever was, having travelled full circle. It remains a rugged coast that conceals hidden dangers and picturesque coves, once exploited by smugglers and wreckers; an industrial past that produced an attractive harbour, a heaven for diverse travellers, and a film set of unbounded opportunities for the cinematographer.

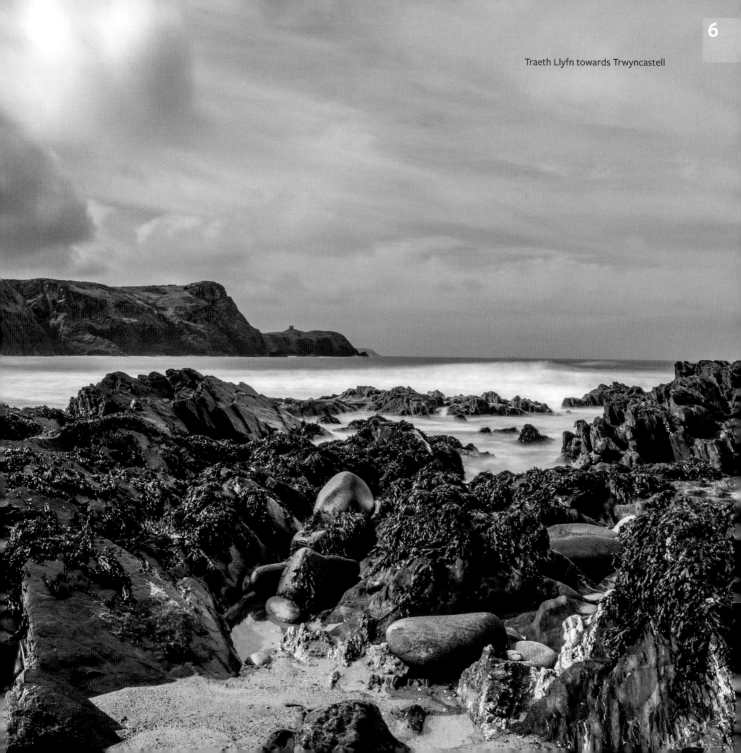

Traeth Llyfn towards Trwyncastell

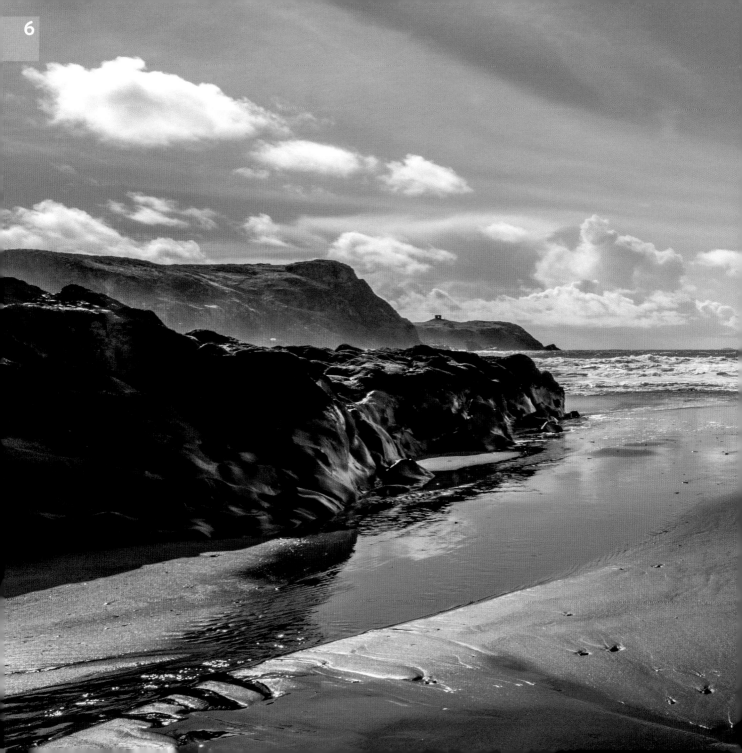

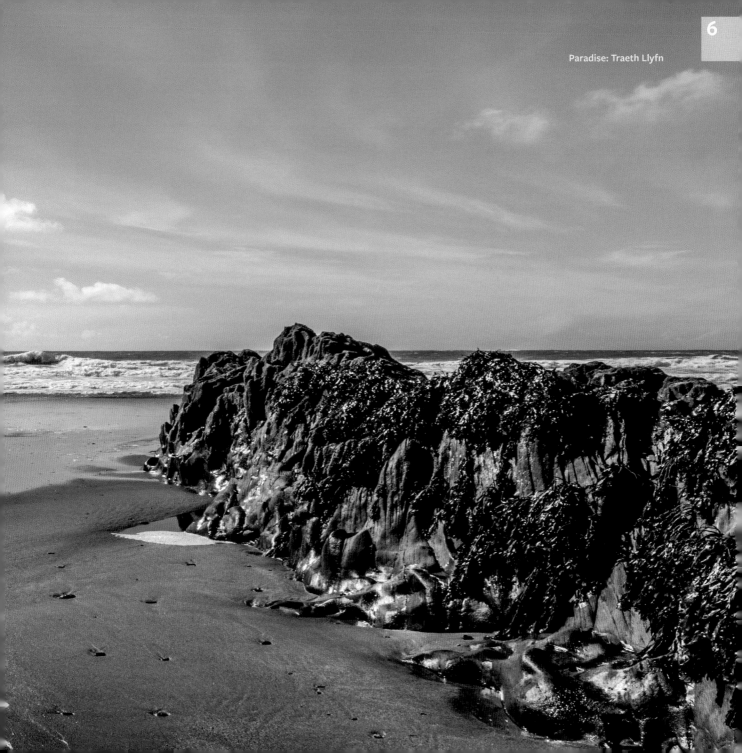

Paradise: Traeth Llyfn

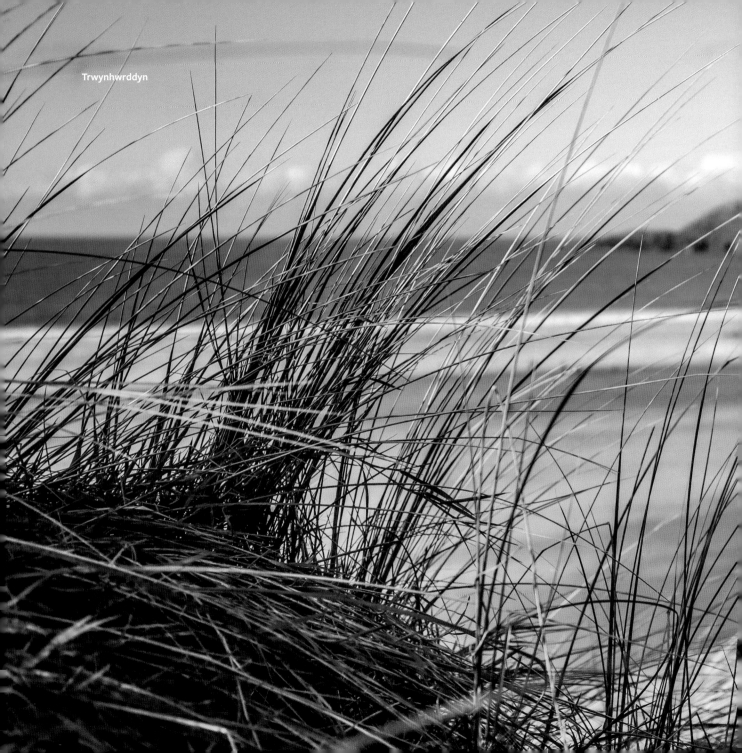
Trwynhwrddyn

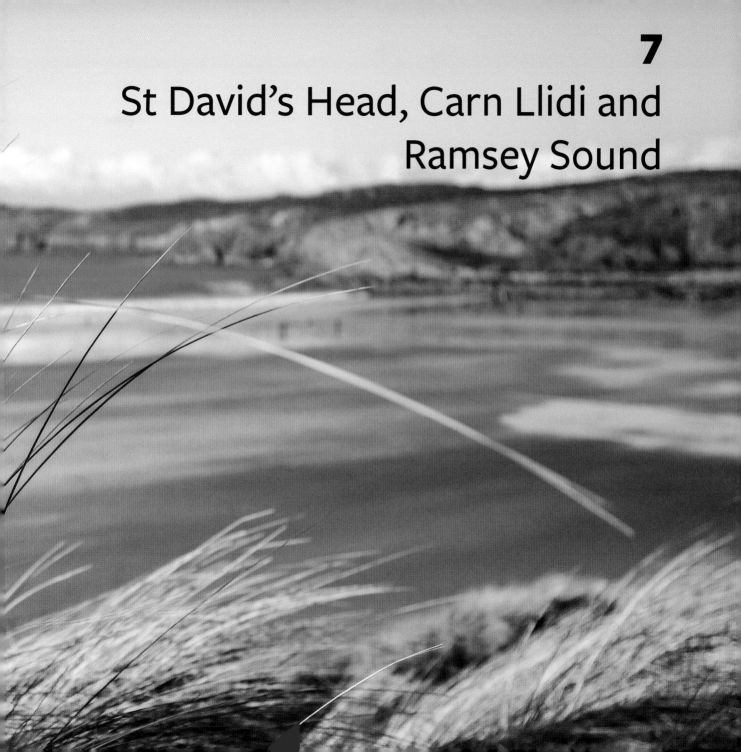

St David's Head, Carn Llidi and Ramsey Sound

Treacherous waters and the legend of druids

THE COASTAL WALK along St David's Head (Penmaen Dewi) is one of the most spectacular in Britain, both in terms of natural beauty and history. Here, blended together on this striking peninsula, is an eclectic tapestry of times gone by.

Whilst the immediate hinterland offered rich rewards to both pirate and invader, the geographical location did not provide easy access. Overlooking the southern limit of the Irish Sea is the strategically positioned site of an Iron Age cliff fort, designed to keep any outsider at bay. Turbulent seas and volcanic rocks that are millions of years old encircle it, thereby providing added protection from physical invasion.

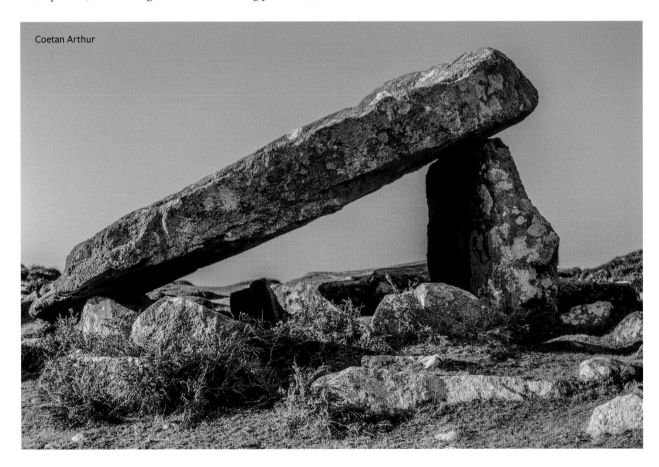

Coetan Arthur

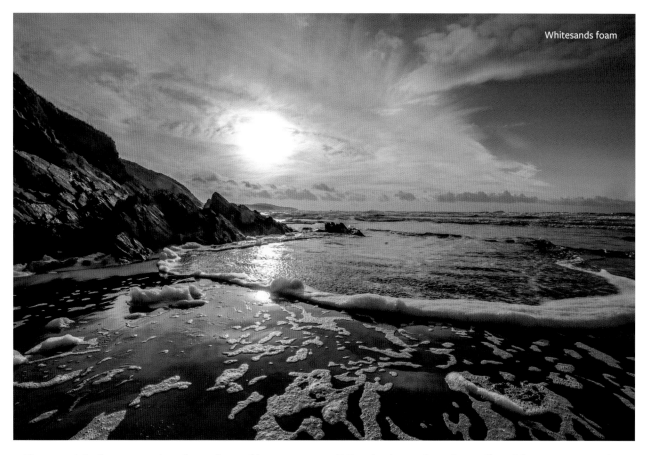

Whitesands foam

Not surprisingly, many an invader and vessel has come to grief in these waters. On 28 November 1788 the *Tarleton*, a 400-ton slaver, foundered off the headland during a voyage from Liverpool to Africa. The international exploitation of slavery was as profitable then as it is today, in the form of human trafficking.

On a more mysterious plane, surrounded by the legend of druids, is the historic site of a Neolithic dolmen or burial chamber known as Coetan Arthur. Built in *c.*3000 BC, today it consists of a small upright stone supporting a sloping capstone. One theory was that it was built to imitate the slope of nearby Carn Llidi. Folklore suggests that King Arthur threw the stones from that ridge.

On a clear day, looking upwards at an expanse of blue sky, the vapour trails produced by the daily flight paths of transatlantic aircraft are visible at regular intervals of fifteen minutes. At altitudes several miles high, every day commercial aircraft fly across the North Atlantic in

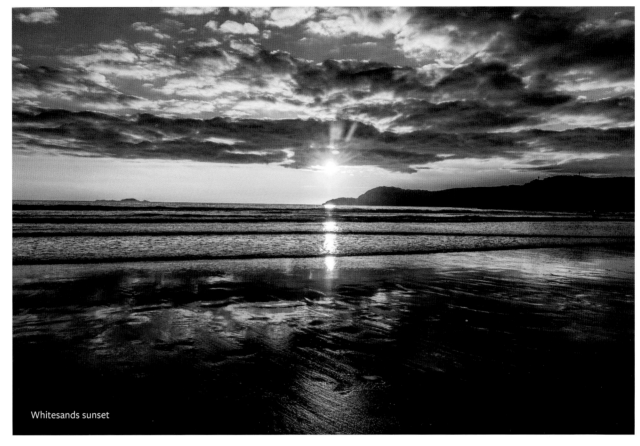

Whitesands sunset

parallel formation of three, travelling the most westerly points on this coastline. The Pembrokeshire coast provides the navigation waypoints to guide air traffic out of the country's sovereign airspace across territorial waters. Those seated in business and economy class, of all creeds and nationalities, fly over an area steeped in history and legend.

Climbing to the top of Carn Llidi (594 ft) provides a panoramic vista of Ramsey Island (Ynys Dewi), the foam-covered sands of Whitesands Bay (Porth Mawr) and, on a clear day, the Wicklow Mountains of Ireland. The landscape around this westerly point reflects the remoteness of the area, with the wild grasses that stretch along the coast framing the snout of Trwynhwrddyn and secluded beaches such as Porthmelgan.

The tranquillity and beauty of the gorgeous sunsets from Whitesands and Lower Treginnis do not prepare a novice seafarer for the treacherous waters that lie ahead in Ramsey Sound. The rocky outcrops known as the Bishops and the Clerks, together with the appropriately named Bitches, guarded by the South Bishop Lighthouse, have been the cause of many shipwrecks. Here there are very powerful tidal currents running through the Sound.

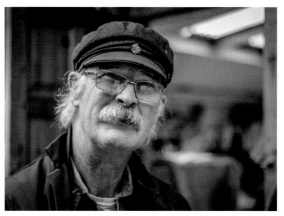

Malcolm Gray

In the early 1950s the farm on Ramsey Island was occupied and worked by Elfed and Melba Griffiths. During the Second World War, Elfed's father Bertie Griffiths was farming here and would make the crossing each week so his son could attend school in St Davids. Elfed would lodge with his grandparents above the Farmers Arms pub, but he yearned to return to the island every weekend to explore and partake in the adventures that Ramsey Island had to offer.

Though the Battle of Britain was being fought by 'the few' of RAF Fighter Command over the skies of southern England during 1940, the fallout was not confined to the English Channel. In 1941, Sgt. Wladyslaw Kiedrzynski, a World War II fighter pilot and a member of 316 Polish Fighter Squadron based at RAF Pembrey in Carmarthenshire, was flying his Hurricane over the area when the engine caught fire, forcing him to bail out off Ramsey Island. Bertie Griffiths responded quickly, showing remarkable courage, and pulled the stranded pilot from the waters, enabling him to go on to make a full recovery. This is but one account of many of farmers in the community assisting in rescuing RAF pilots who had got into difficulties off the coast of Pembrokeshire.

Today, there are expeditions running from St Justinian, taking tourists on exhilarating adventures to Ramsey Island and beyond. It is also the home of the St Davids Lifeboat Station. A new station was built in 2016 and today sits side-by-side with the old one, looking towards Ramsey Island.

Whilst Pembrokeshire has witnessed invaders of one kind or another committing acts of piracy and wholesale theft, included in the category of criminals at work in the county must also be the local smugglers and the seemingly upright members of the community. At the slightest whisper of an opportunity, they too have taken swift advantage and have callously plundered shipwrecks around the coast. Many of these accounts are well documented, whilst knowledge of the more obscure incidents can be gained from speaking to the few remaining old sages around St Davids, who have a wealth of stories. Former coxswain Malcolm Gray is one of the few able to recount such tales.

On 16 December 1668 the *Amity*, sailing from Southampton, foundered in a storm in the treacherous waters of Ramsey Sound. When the anchors failed, the vessel ran ashore and locals plundered her cargo of wine and fruit. In 1770, local smugglers even had the nerve to attack and scuttle a government-owned vessel called the *Pelham Cutter*, off St Davids. It was attacked by the crew of a wherry, who plundered everything on board.

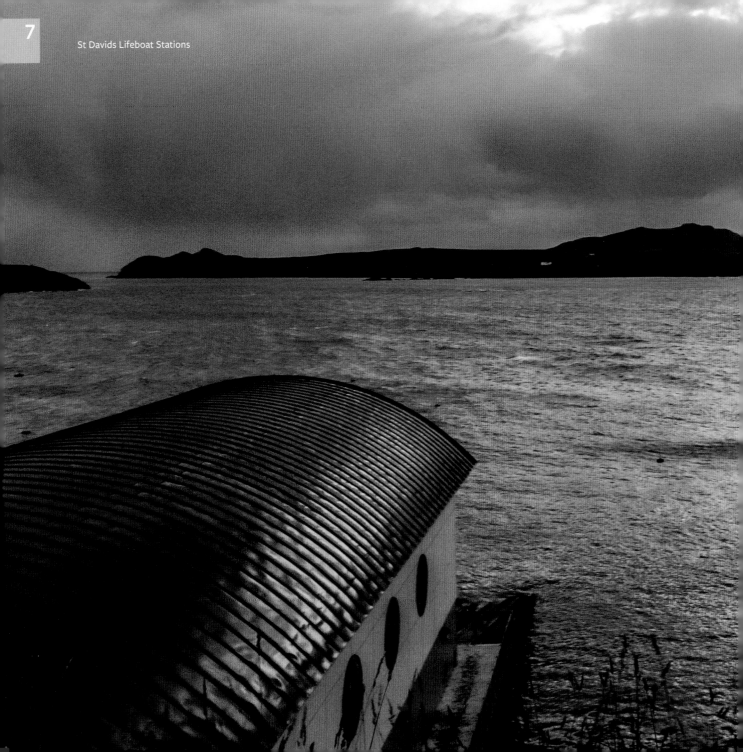

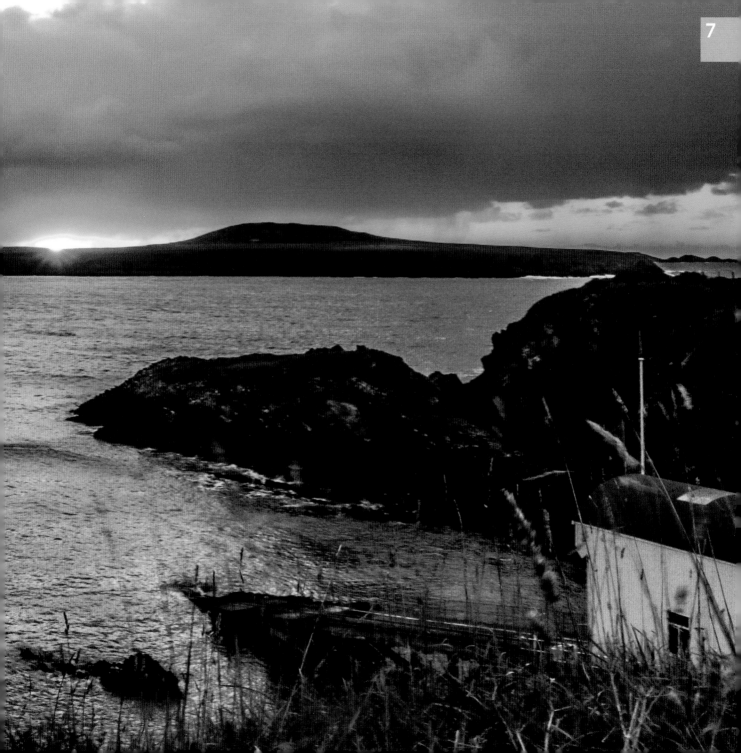

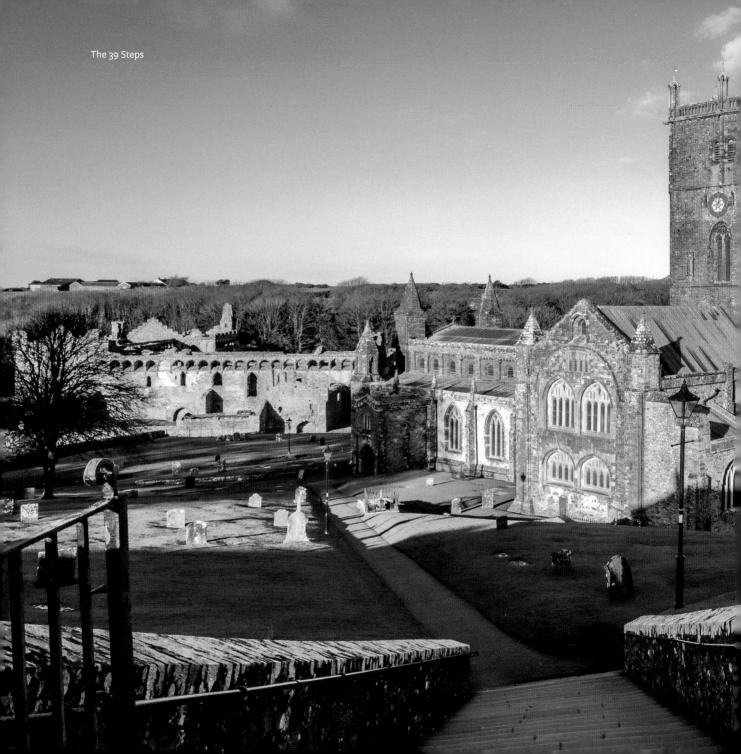

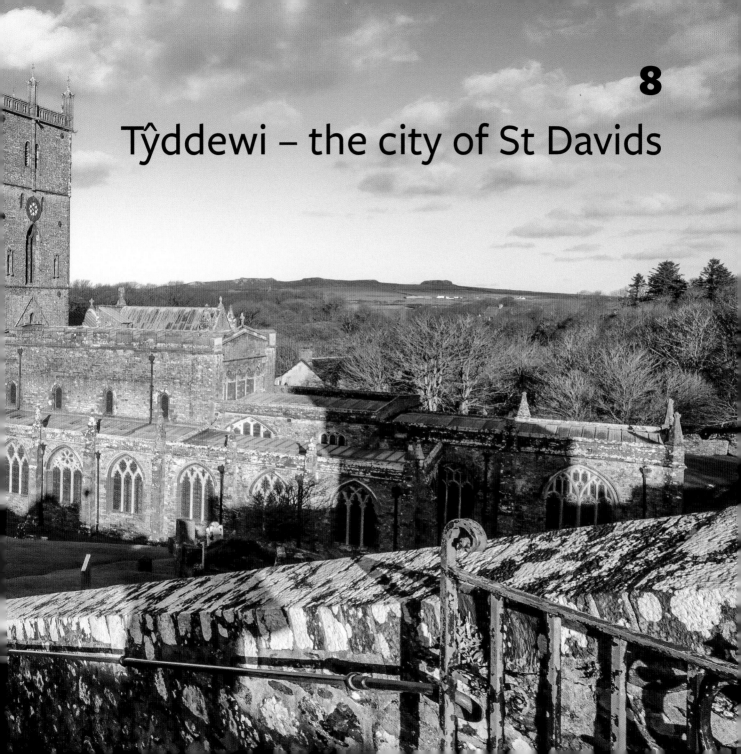

Tŷddewi – the city of St Davids

Piety, desecration and solitude

S
T DAVIDS IS today a popular destination for tourists from all over the world, or for those who simply seek to escape city life and find solitude. Whilst enjoying an air of serenity, the smallest city in the UK hides a difficult past, blighted by troublesome interlopers and an incumbent preying upon its riches for personal gain.

Many of the churches and chapels throughout the county hark back to the days of the seafaring Celtic saints who brought Christianity to Wales from Ireland, and those who followed. The magnificent St Davids Cathedral was built upon the site of the monastic community founded by Saint David (Dewi Sant), Abbot of Menevia – the previous name for St Davids – in the sixth century. The building of the current cathedral commenced in 1181, the Vikings having destroyed the previous structures. Vikings often made raids from the westerly waters around the county looking for plunder. Though the cathedral had been built in a valley out of sight of marauders, in AD 999 Bishop Morgennau was murdered by Vikings, and Bishop Abraham suffered a similar fate in 1080.

With its blend of Romanesque and Gothic architecture, the current Cathedral is rich in history. In the twelfth century, Pope Calixtus II decreed that the shrine of St David was so sacred that two pilgrimages to this most westerly point of Pembrokeshire was equivalent to one to Rome; and three were equivalent to one pilgrimage to Jerusalem. In 1648 during the Civil War, when Oliver Cromwell was in the south of the county laying siege to Pembroke Castle, his Parliamentarian soldiers destroyed much of the building, taking valuable lead.

The Bishop's Palace, adjacent to the Cathedral, was not impervious to a bishop himself intent on plunder and destruction. In 1538, at the beginning of the Reformation, Bishop William Barlow, its incumbent, stripped the lead from the roof to pay for the dowries of his five daughters. Ever since, it has remained in a state of disrepair, a living monument to desecration.

Today, the Cathedral precinct remains a destination for pilgrims and for those wishing to engage in educational and spiritual activities. Similarly, St Non's Bay – named after the mother of St David, who according to legend gave birth to the patron saint on a clifftop during a great storm around AD 462 – provides solace. A ruined chapel and a holy well, said to possess miraculous healing powers, mark the supposed site of the saint's birth. The Passionate Fathers built St Non's Retreat in 1929, whilst the modern Chapel of our Lady & St Non was built five years later in the early Celtic style by Cecil Morgan-Griffiths, a solicitor from Carmarthen (Caerfyrddin), who used stone salvaged from nearby local historic sites.

On a secular note, George Llewellyn, formerly of Tygwyn, Whitesands, St Davids, was said to have amassed a fortune from smuggling, and built the windmill at Twr y Felin in 1806 from the profits of contraband. He is said to have *'got his money on the water and invested it on the wind'*. In 1866, the tower having suffered storm damage, David Evans of Treiago Farm repaired and renovated the structure using materials from a shipwreck. In 1940, due to the formidable and remorseless presence of other invaders in our airspace, namely the German Luftwaffe, evacuees from the London Blitz were accommodated at Twr y Felin. Today it is described as a luxury contemporary art hotel, featuring over 100 original artworks commissioned to represent the St Davids Peninsula and Pembrokeshire.

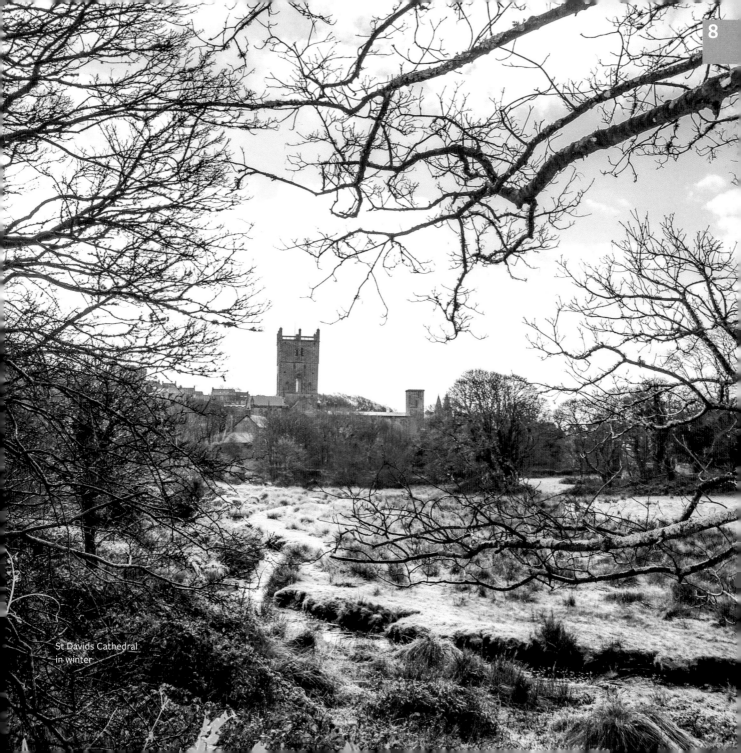

St Davids Cathedral in winter

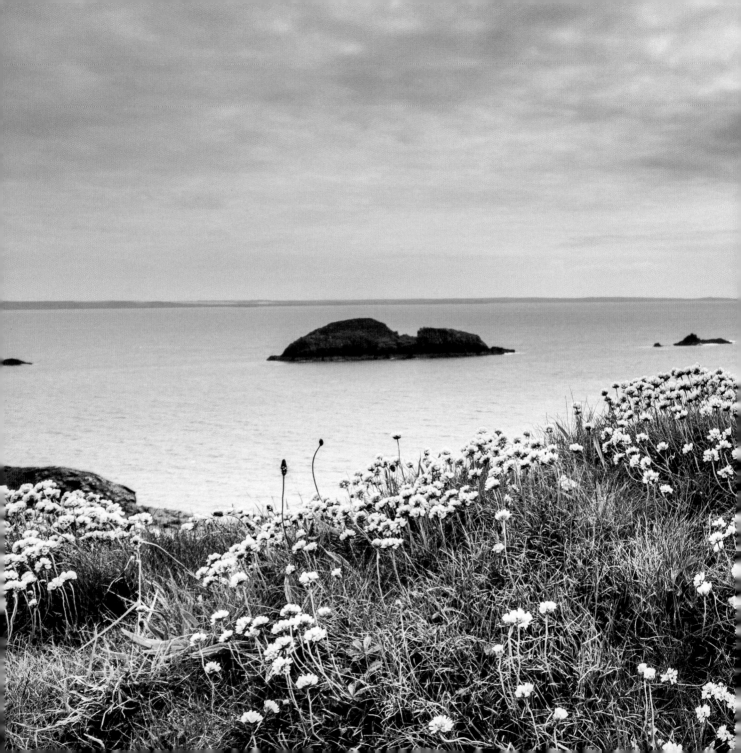

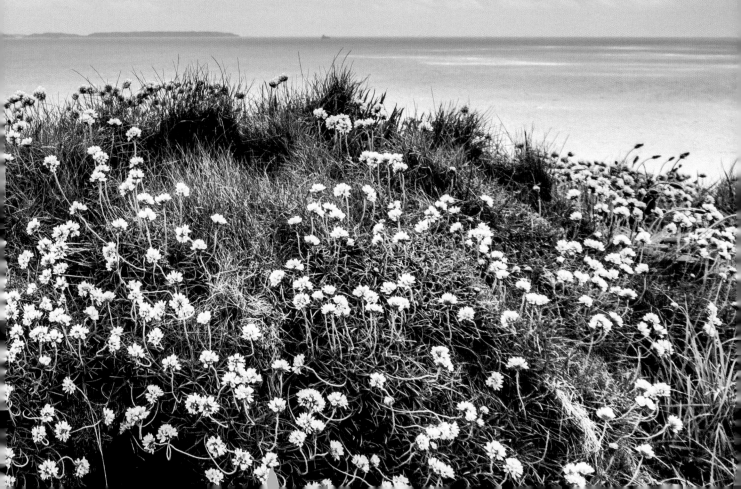

9

St Brides Bay, Solva and Brandy Brook

Smuggling, wrecking – the last frontier

T HE COASTAL PATH from St Davids to Solva (Solfach) provides a magnificent outlook over the mouth of St Brides Bay (Bae Sain Ffraid). The view takes in some seven miles of beautiful coastal scenery where hundreds of vessels met their end and where their wrecks can still be located. Many came to grief in these waters, only to be salvaged by local folk for the valuable commodities on board that had failed to reach port. They were also plundered for timber, to be installed into the affluent residences of dignitaries in the community.

As well as being a busy transatlantic shipping lane with links to Ireland, Liverpool and New York, the area saw the presence of the Fleet Air Arm in the 1940s. The experience of two World Wars also left the seabed around the

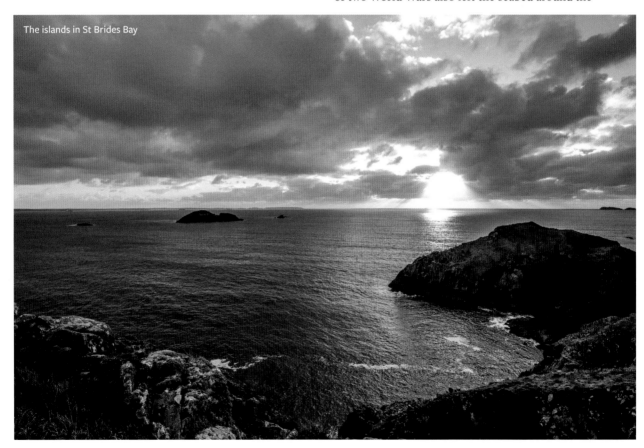

The islands in St Brides Bay

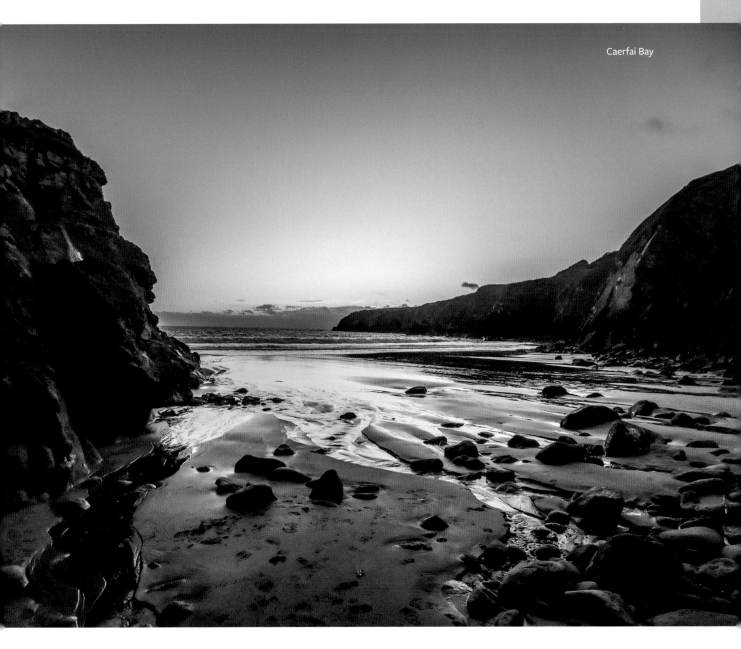

Caerfai Bay

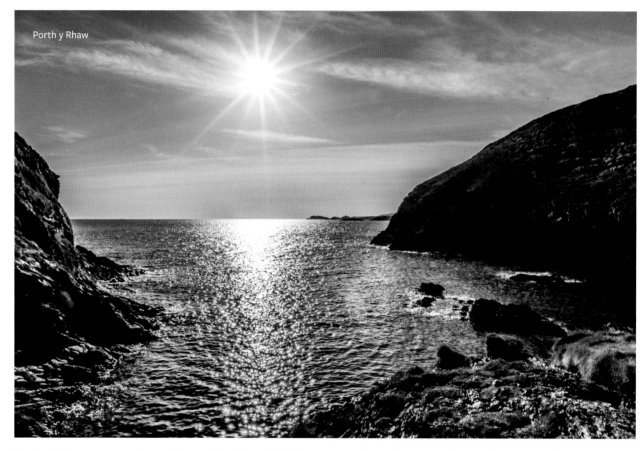

Porth y Rhaw

Pembrokeshire coast replete with vessels either shelled by visitations from the Luftwaffe or torpedoed by U-boats.

The islands of Skomer (Ynys Sgomer) and Skokholm (Ynys Sgogwm) are constantly visible along this section of the Wales Coast Path. Both were named by invading Vikings. In days before environmental and scientific agencies focused on this part of the United Kingdom, Skomer and Skokholm provided smugglers with a place to hide their booty, in particular brandy and tallow.

Lying to the west is the smaller island of Grassholm (Gwales), conspicuous for the distinctive flash of white guano running across its face. It is one of the world's largest colonies and breeding sites for northern gannets, with over 35,000 pairs. Seals bask on the rocks surrounding the island whilst harbour porpoise and dolphins are regular sightings.

Standing in distant isolation some 26 miles out to sea is the Smalls Lighthouse, the most westerly point of Wales.

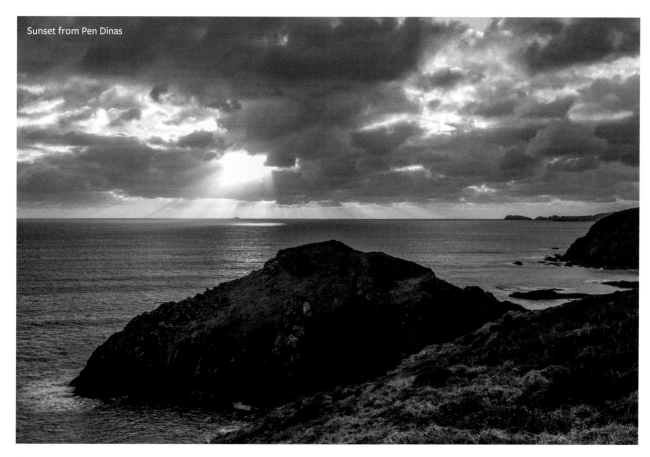

Sunset from Pen Dinas

The current lighthouse was completed in 1861, replacing an earlier structure originally built on Solva Quay during the winter of 1775–76. It can be seen standing erect between Grassholm and Ramsey (Ynys Dewi). In 2016 Chris Crow directed *The Lighthouse*, depicting the dark psychological drama of two lighthouse keepers, Thomas Griffiths and Thomas Howell, played by Mark Lewis Jones and Michael Jibson respectively, driven to madness and the accidental death of one when stranded for months on the Smalls by a freak storm. When Howell thought he would be accused of the murder of Griffiths, he strapped his corpse to the side of the lighthouse. This bleak real-life event of the early nineteenth century led to Trinity House ensuring that there was always a roster of three keepers on duty before automation took over in the 1980s.

Heading towards the hamlets of Caer Bwdy (known locally as Caerbwdi) and Trelerw, and along Morfa Common to Porth y Rhaw, you see some of the most

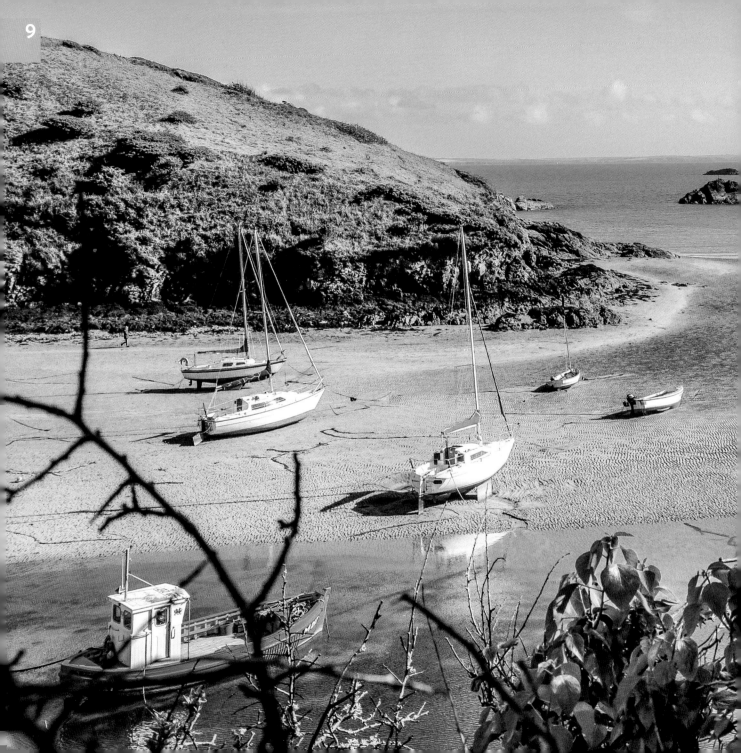

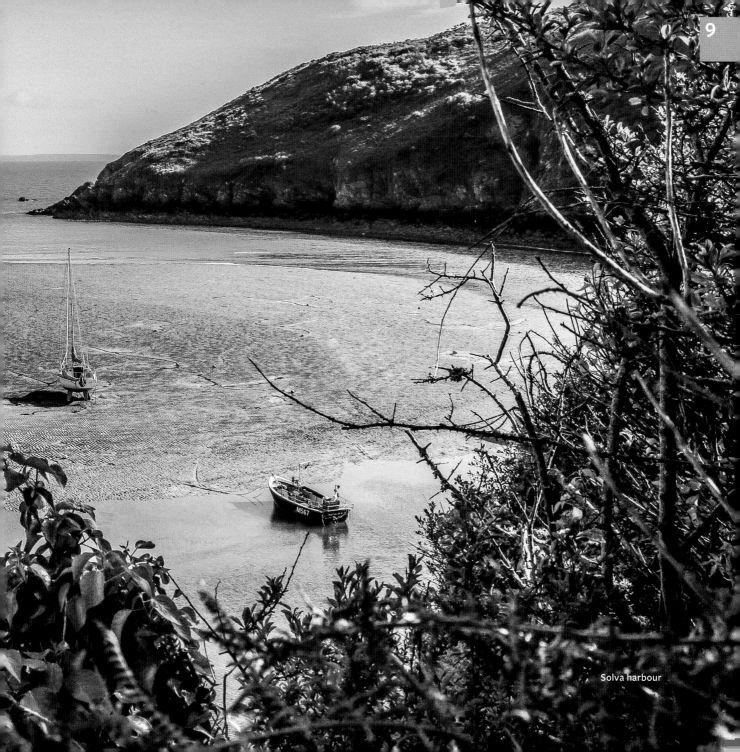

Solva harbour

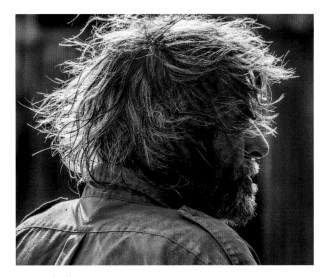

Drowned Sailor

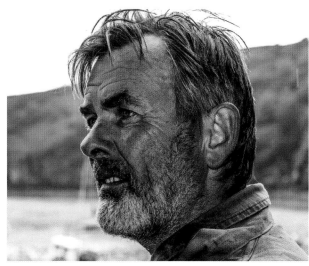

Local fisherman

interesting rock strata on this stretch of the coastal path. At Caerbwdi the remains of an old corn mill stand with millstones and a square lime kiln, harking back to days when the indigenous population were self sufficient and not reliant upon imports. Porth y Rhaw is at the mouth of a meltwater channel flanked by steep gradients. At the head of the valley during medieval times there were previously nine holy wells where the visiting sick derived comfort and relief (Nine Wells/Naw Ffynon).

The area is replete with caves that look out onto St Brides Bay, concealing a myriad of hideouts where illicit activities associated with smuggling were rife. 'Ogof Tobacco' is only accessible from the sea, and as the name implies, it was a cave used by smugglers' to hide the once lucrative commodity. There was apparently an underground passageway leading to Llanunwas Manor, lying on the boundary of the village of Solva.

On 1 November 1679, the *Santa Cruz* ran aground in St Brides Bay and has never been found. She was carrying gold and is much sought after by divers, as are many of the wrecks that remain undiscovered.

The picturesque village of Solva was once renowned for underground passages where contraband goods from local wrecks were concealed and hoarded. The nineteenth century is full of folk tales of local dignitaries and respectable members of the community engaged in smuggling activities – some mythical, some true.

In one case, Raymond of Bank House, who was a local Justice of the Peace and a merchant with a strong financial interest in trading activities in Solva, was alerted to the presence of a vessel in the harbour carrying a cargo of contraband salt. Finding himself in this invidious position, he gave advance warning to local fishermen that he was aware of the situation, by which time the incriminating evidence and the smugglers had vanished. On another occasion, a Customs Officer in attendance at evening service at Solva Baptist Chapel (Capel Bach), became inquisitive when he saw that the faces of the congregation were particularly well illuminated. When he discovered that the light came from numerous candles that had been made from tallow smuggled into Solva harbour, they were immediately confiscated as smuggled goods. Those in attendance left the service in darkness.

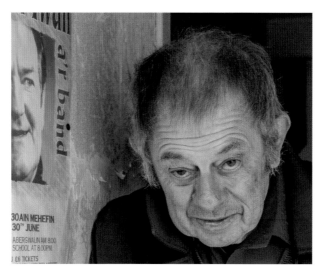

'Dai the Bomb'

On 18 October 1981, three Greek tugs – *Veronicos Alexia*, *Veronicos Georgios* and *Veronicos Barbara IV* – ran aground beneath the cliffs at this location, instigating a number of profitable salvage exercises, characteristically conducted by people frrom the area.

In 2014, film producer Kevin Allen set the fictional seaside village of Llareggub in Solva for his production of a new and quirky version of Dylan Thomas' *Under Milk Wood*. This invasion throughout June by a large cast and production team was welcomed, not just attracting the curious but providing work for many living in the area. It also relied heavily upon the hospitality of local residents. Many local characters from the village were used as extras, playing the role of sailors (drunken or drowned) or the walking dead.

The cast and crew used the The Ship Inn in Lower Solva for their wardrobe facilities and some memorable scenes were shot there. Frondeg House was transformed into The Sailors Arms and the hamlet of Solfach Draw was used as the set for a variety of scenes, with actors Rhys Ifans, Sharon Morgan, Charlotte Church and Sue Roderick as their mainstay. The imposing Fort was also used in a number of scenes, as was Solva Quay, and the old Lifeboat Station was converted into a church to film an unconventional wedding scene.

Over the years the village of Solva has been home to many memorable characters, many long gone. One celebrated character who lived his whole life in Solva was the late David Evans, popularly known as 'Dai the Bomb'. The epithet results from his deep association with the CND movement when it was in its prime, and his participation in the Aldermaston marches in the early 1960s. He championed the campaign against nuclear war in Pembrokeshire whilst the anti-war activist Bertrand Russell advocated the cause throughout the world.

Many visitors return time and again. One who has a long association with Wales, and in particular St David's Peninsula, from the early 1970s is Welsh-speaking Patagonian singer René Griffiths. When his ancestors disembarked from the *Mimosa* at Puerto Madryn in 1865, little did they think that René would seek an education at Coleg Harlech, studying Welsh Literature, and frequently

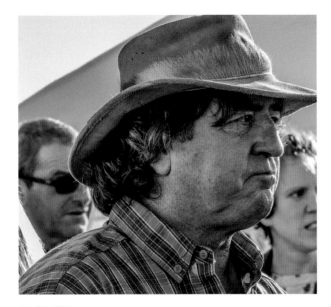

René Griffiths

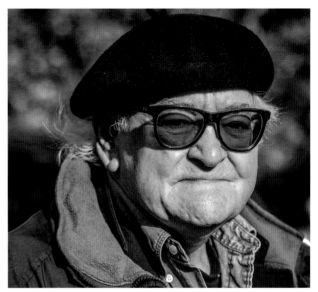

Meic Stevens

return to Wales whenever the opportunity arose. He has been a regular visitor to Solva and doubtless feels at home when speaking the Welsh language at the annual Edge Festival held in August, or when feeding Alan Davies' South American alpacas in the secluded valley at Middle Mill (Felin Ganol). Cult Welsh-language singer Meic Stevens, 'the Welsh Bob Dylan', also hails from the village – his mother Betty was a talented musician too.

Passing the historic limekilns, from the period when lime was a lucrative asset in building and agriculture, the ascent meets the narrow spine of the Gribin. At its summit there was once an Iron Age Fort and settlement, and there are views of the Green Scar and Black Rock islands.

Apparently the waters around these small islands were so treacherous that the Vikings were deterred from entering the inlet. It was created by glacial erosion, and

is actually a fjord, ironically a common sight on the Scandinavian coast. The descent onto the beach at Gwadn meets the steep incline above Porth y Bwch.

On 8 January 1773 at this location, the *Phoebe and Peggy* ran aground whilst sailing from Philadelphia to Liverpool, near to the entrance to Solva harbour. This beach below Dinas Fawr proved difficult to access, but that did not deter the community around Solva. Over 60 people drowned, and bodies washed up on shore were stripped and plundered. A ballad subsequently written by a local man referred to the callous activities of two men, named John Phillip and Luke Davey, who robbed one of the perished, a woman known as Madam Elliott, of 500 guineas before cutting the rings from her fingers and splitting her ears to steal her earrings. All the bodies recovered from the beach were buried a few miles away at Brawdy Church.

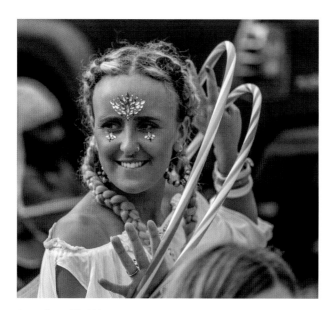

A reveller at The Edge

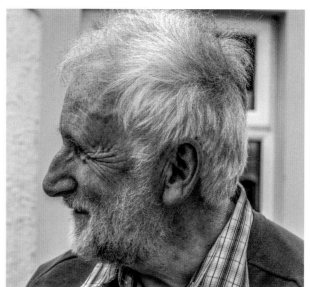

Alan Davies

Going inland, the Baptist chapels of Blaenllyn and Newton 'are blessed' with materials sourced from smuggled timbers and flotsam washed up in Newgale (Niwgwl) and Whitesands (Porth Mawr). These were used to build the gallery, pillars and windows in 1842 and 1862 respectively.

The path to Newgale is at times arduous: an up-and-down trudge through fields occupied by livestock. There are many picturesque coves after passing through St Elvis (Llaneilfyw). Porthmynawyd Beach is well off the tourist trail and leads to Pointz Castle, which was once a motte and bailey named after Poncius – another Norman invader; in this case a knight.

Before the descent into Newgale is the village at the head of the valley, aptly named Penycwm, in the parish of Brawdy. The name Brawdy is a corruption of the

Welsh name for the village, Breudeth, which appears to be a derivation of the saint's name 'Bridget'. Penycwm traditionally represented the last vestige of any Welsh-speaking community, Welsh place name and Welsh accent before crossing the Landsker frontier at Brandy Brook and arriving at Newgale. The percentage of Welsh speakers in the area according to the 1891 census was 88%. By 1971 it had dropped to 36% and the 2011 census revealed that just 19.1% of the population could speak Welsh.

Between 1944 and 1992, Brawdy – insignificant as it may have been considered by locals – was ranked to be of such strategic importance that it was variously occupied by the Fleet Air Arm, the Royal Navy and the Royal Air Force, and saw thousands of recruits brought together from all over the United Kingdom. In the 1970s the United States Navy established an oceanographic research centre at the site.

St Brides Bay | Solva | Brandy Brook **81**

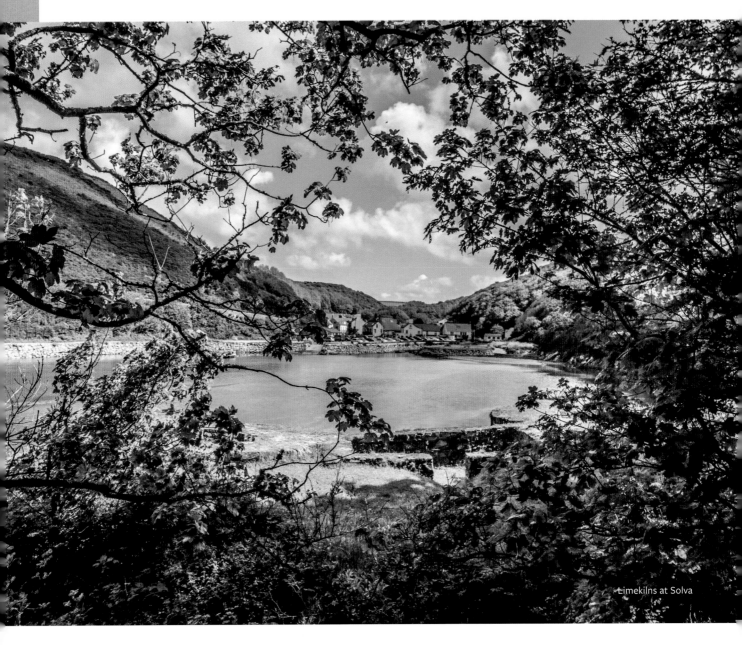

Limekilns at Solva

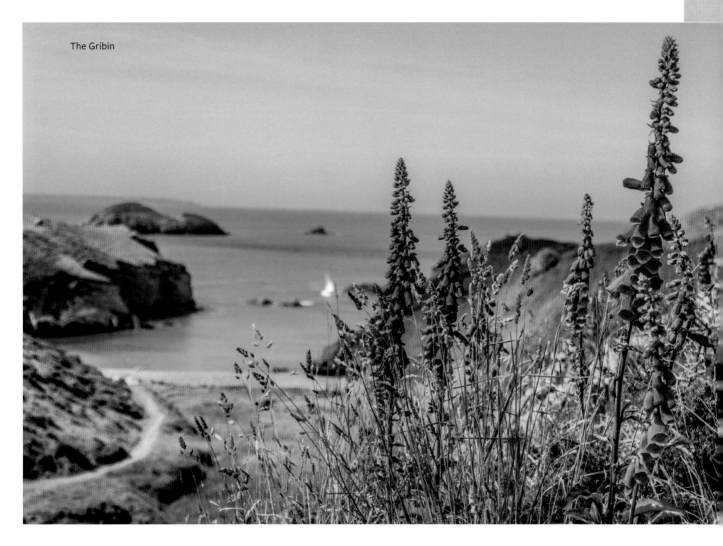

The Gribin

In 1995 the British Army took over what became Cawdor Barracks, now occupied by the Royal Regiment of Signals (Electronic Warfare).

Though thousands of outside military personnel moved into the county and passed through this site as part of essential training for armed conflict over those years, they promoted the economy of Pembrokeshire and enhanced the business sector. The area reaped immediate benefits. The Search and Rescue Sea King Helicopter was literally a lifesaver for those in distress in the seas

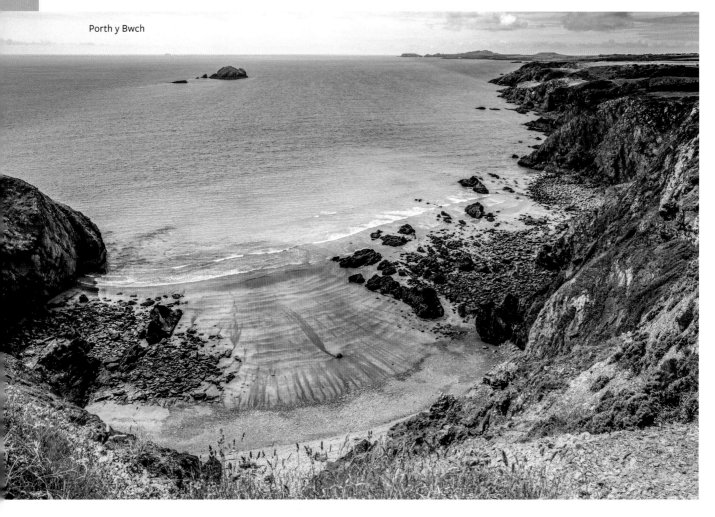

Porth y Bwch

off Pembrokeshire and further afield, before eventually departing from Brawdy in 1994. The people of the county owe a debt of gratitude to the many hands that came to the rescue of 'those in peril on the sea'.

Local schools, particularly Ysgol Dewi Sant, saw an influx of children of military personnel from Brawdy, who had very English accents and had lived in Malta, Cyprus, Germany and the Far East. Though they were greeted with understandable scepticism at first, they very soon blended in with the majority of pupils and some made their homes in the county, settling here with their families.

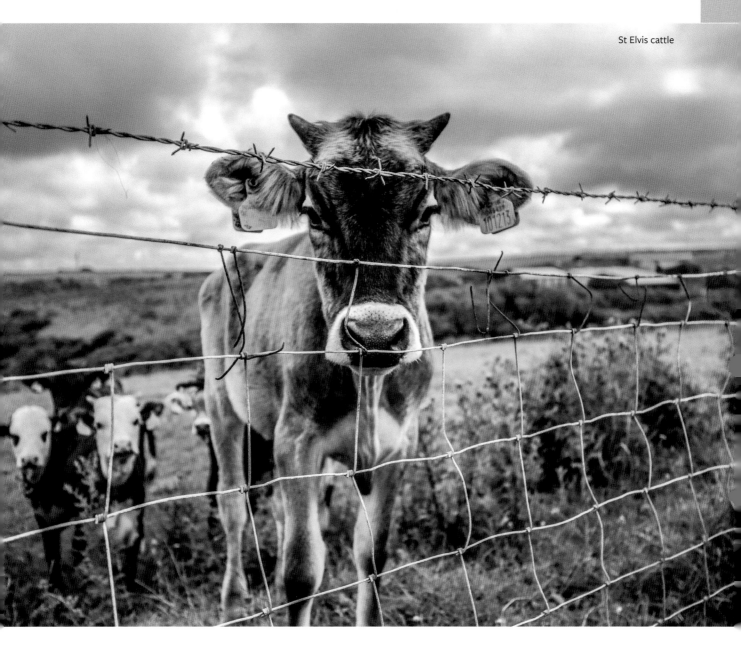

St Elvis cattle

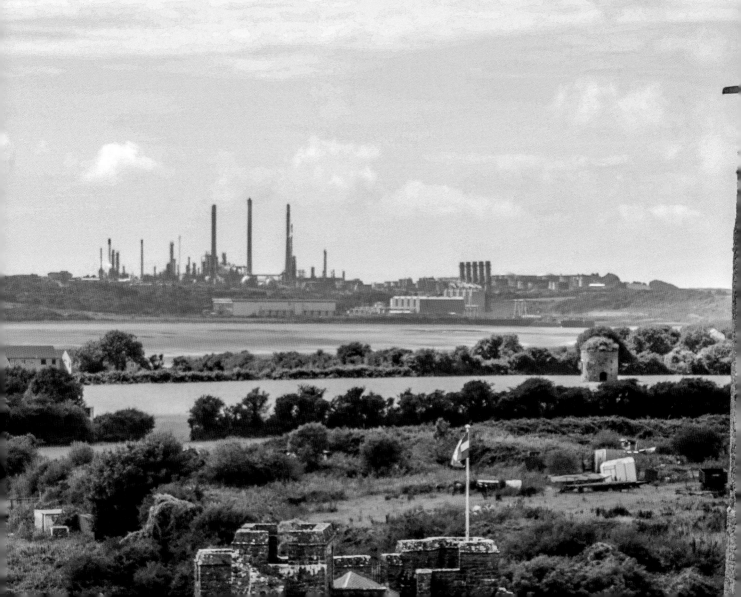

SECTION 2
SOUTH OF THE LANDSKER

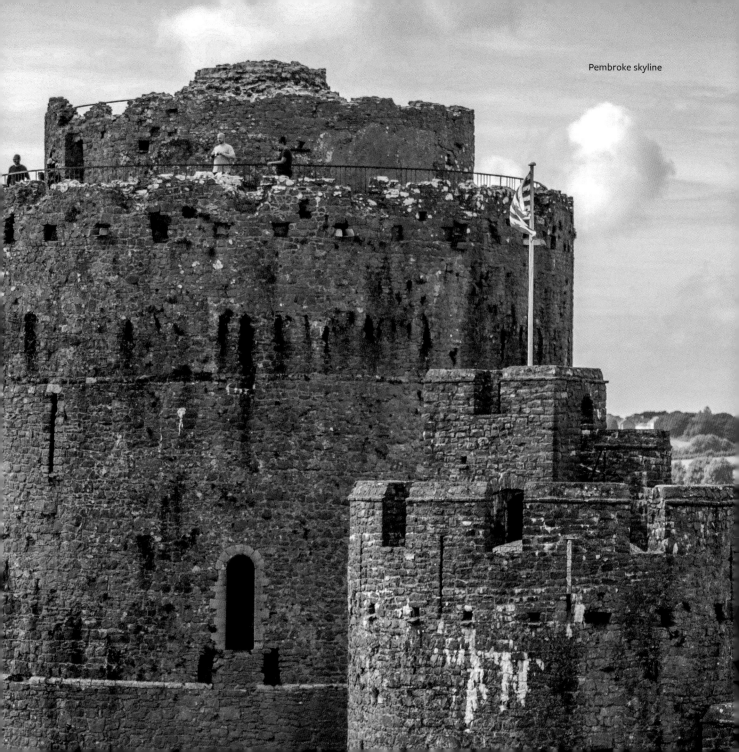

Pembroke skyline

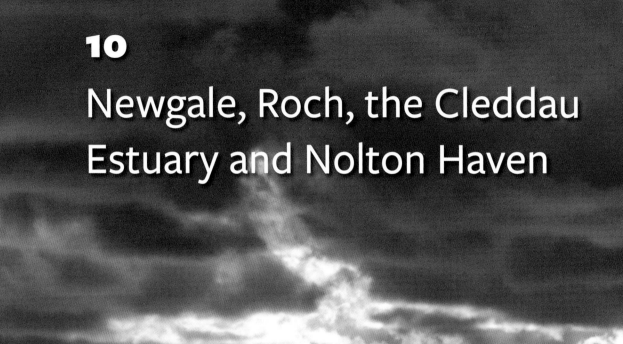

10

Newgale, Roch, the Cleddau Estuary and Nolton Haven

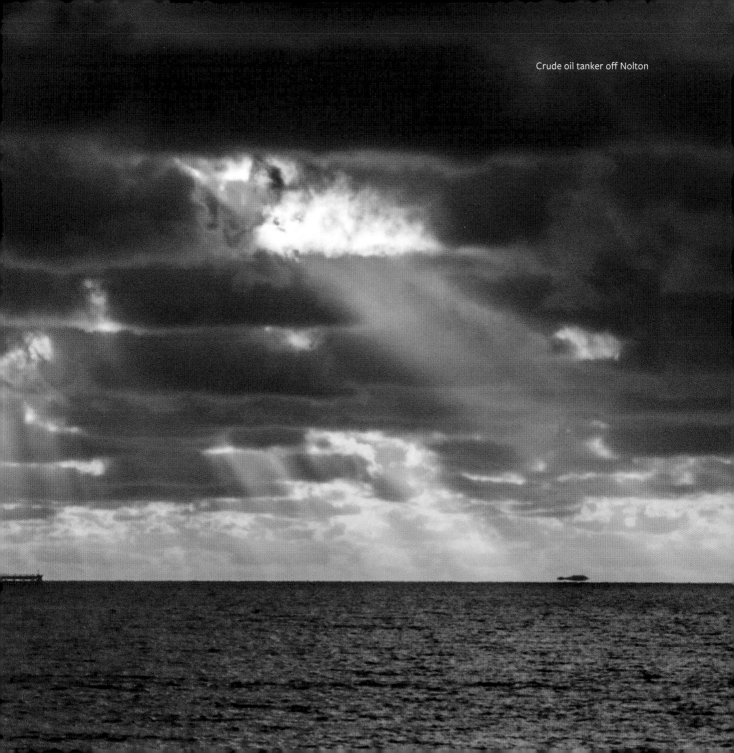

Crude oil tanker off Nolton

Vikings, Normans and Flemings

THE TRANSITION THAT follows on leaving Penycwm and crossing the hidden Landsker demarcation was once comparable to switching wavelengths from Radio Cymru to Radio 2. That boundary has today softened, though it does continue to signal a cultural and linguistic divide. Industry and commerce have left a heavier mark upon the south of the county, but this is tamed by natural beauty. The language spoken today is a hybrid of Welsh and English, but further south the native tongue ceases to be dominant.

Newgale (Niwgwl) is in the parish of Roch (Y Garn), and running into the sea there is Brandy Brook. The name has an association with contraband spirit and smuggling activity. This windswept surfers' paradise of tumultuous waves along two miles of sands – separated from the road by a mountain of collapsing pebbles – is bracing, to put it mildly. In winter the seawater forms a natural lake, whereas in the summer months, campers invade and make their home under idyllic sunsets.

The Great Storm of 1703 washed away the old pub, The Bridge Inn, which once stood on the storm beach at Newgale. Today the Duke of Edinburgh, built on the other side of the pebbles, has replaced it. The sea had claimed another victim in 1690 when the *Resolution*, a fully rigged ship, was blown ashore at Newgale and the wreck plundered by locals.

Once more the county was to witness intruders from outside its boundaries who for malign reasons sought to exploit the geography of the area, quite unbeknown to the local population. During 1989–90 St Brides Bay (Bae Sain Ffraid) was the hideout for a secret arms cache associated with terrorist activities. 'Operation Pebble' was a seven-week stakeout at Newgale that resulted in convictions at the Old Bailey and prison sentences of 30 years.

Travelling inland towards the county town of Haverfordwest (Hwlffwrdd), the A487 passes Roch Castle, which occupies an elevated position along the Landsker divide. This was once part of the De La Roche Estate that extended south to Llangwm, and was garrisoned for the Royalist cause during the Civil War until besieged in 1644. It represents just one link in a chain of castles built by the Norman invaders.

Going south from Newgale, the coast path passes Rickets Head, once part of the small Pembrokeshire coalfield. Between 1850 and 1905 several collieries exploited seams of anthracite that ran beneath the sea on this part of the coast. Collieries such as Southwood (Farm) and Simpson (Cross) are long-forgotten coalfields where seams were abandoned but old shafts remain. Vessels carrying coal were often shipwrecked but were of little interest to the astute smuggler. In this corner of the country, coal was of little value as an attraction in comparison to such commodities as brandy, whisky, salt and tallow, where the profits from onward supply were that much greater.

The Daugleddau Estuary is where the Eastern and Western Cleddau rivers unite. It is at the hub of the county, and its historic occupation by outside forces has played a significant part in shaping the county. The area flanking the River Cleddau on its eastern branch was the subject of industrial exploitation from 1800 onwards. At Landshipping, over 10,000 tons of coal was being produced annually. Further development, with fatal consequences, occurred when the pit was expanded under the river. On 14 February 1844 some 40 miners, including

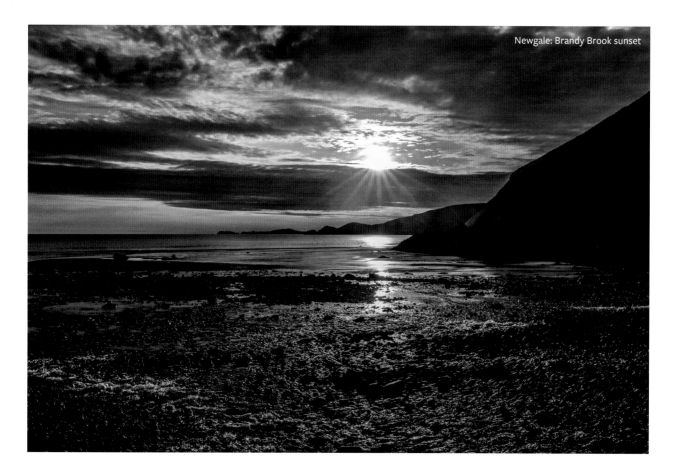

Newgale: Brandy Brook sunset

women and children employed illegally, were drowned while working a section never previously mined at high tide, when the pressure of the water breached the roof and flooded the mine.

The village of Llangwm on the Cleddau's western bank was once a winter retreat for invading Vikings, where they would put their longships ashore for repair in a safe haven. They left their stamp on the area and named the location Langheim, meaning Long Road. They also settled to the north at Freystrop, which comes from 'Freya', the Norse goddess of love, and 'thorpe', meaning village or hamlet.

One of the consequences of the later Norman Conquest was the colonisation of areas on the coast of Pembrokeshire and further inland. Noblemen who had been part of this successful invasive force on the south coast of England were rewarded with lands far to the west, and were reputed to have deployed English-speaking farm labourers from Gloucester and Somerset to cultivate

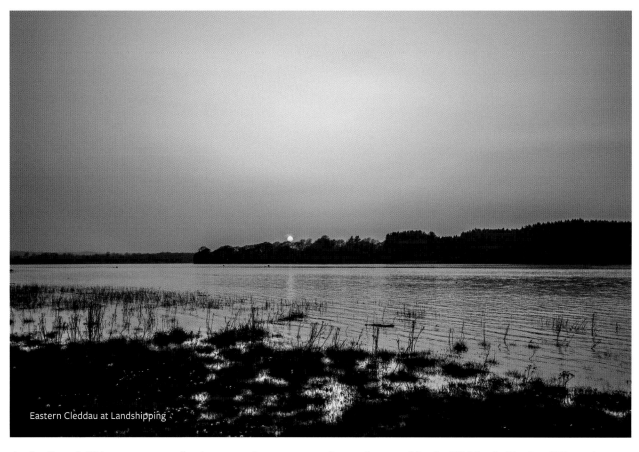

Eastern Cleddau at Landshipping

the fertile soil. This may account for the unusual accent prevalent here. The Normans built a series of motte and bailey fortifications that developed into impressive castles along a 'line' bisecting the county into north and south, in order to keep the Welsh in check.

The most important of all Landsker castles, and strategically placed further to the east, is Llawhaden. Originally built by the Normans in the twelfth century and mentioned by Giraldus Cambrensis (Gerald of Wales),

it was destroyed by the Welsh – led by Lord Rhys – in 1193, before the return of English rule early the following century and the building during the fourteenth century of the structure whose remains can still be seen today.

As well as the frontier defences across the county, the Norman style of architecture is evident in the many churches that were built in this period. This again, was quite alien to the indigenous peoples of Pembrokeshire.

It was during the twelfth century that Flemish peoples

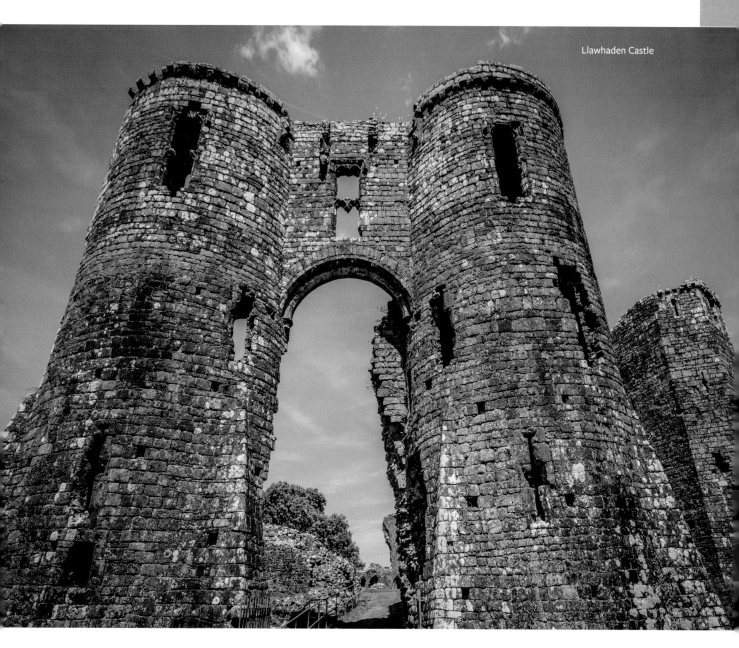

Llawhaden Castle

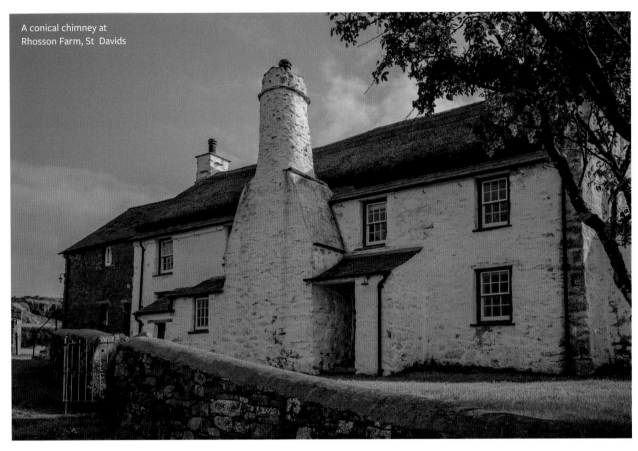

A conical chimney at
Rhosson Farm, St Davids

(from what was then Flanders, now in modern-day Belgium) were forced to escape devastating floods (1106) in the Low Countries and seek refuge in England, with whom they had strong commercial links through the wool trade. They had also formed an alliance with William of Normandy as a result of his marriage to Matilda, Princess of Flanders, and provided skilful foot soldiers as part of the Norman invasion of England in 1066.

Initially welcomed by the English natives, friction soon developed when they started to feel that the country was being overrun by Flemings.

Henry I (King of England from 1100–1135) adopted a two-pronged strategy, to resolve the dilemma of English xenophobia and also ensure allegiance to the King in Wales. It was decided that some 2,500 of England's incomers should migrate to Pembrokeshire, where a colony of Flemish peoples settled in the south of the county. They established themselves in what were originally the cantrefs of Rhos and Deugleddyf (Daugleddau) on the Cleddau Estuary, and in the western commote of Castell Hu (Cas-wis or Wiston), formerly part of ancient Dyfed. In return for being rewarded with stolen lands in the area, the Flemings were deployed to suppress recurrent Welsh rebellion.

Described as 'Flemish Wolves', they savagely repressed the Welsh people by driving them from their homes into the north of the county and permanently transformed the character of the area by introducing major Flemish settlements, described by historians as 'planted towns'. Many place names in the county can be so attributed. The village of Wiston is associated with Wizo the Fleming and another refugee from Flanders, Letard Litelking, founded the rural community of Letterston. Pembrokeshire Records insist that the Flemish leader Tancred (who married Gerald of Wales' aunt) built Haverfordwest Castle in 1108, though some attribute this to the Englishman Gilbert de Clare, Marcher Earl of Pembroke, appointed by the king to guard the border between England and Wales. The hamlet of Tancredston lies in rich farmland a few miles north-west of Haverfordwest.

Though Flemish craftsmen undoubtedly made a contribution to the architecture of some of the churches, whether they can be credited with the appearance of 'Flemish chimneys' or 'conical chimneys' within the county is a matter of debate. A classic example of the Flemish chimney is to be found at Rhosson Uchaf – albeit north of the Landsker, just outside St Davids. It was here that the archaeologist and historian Richard Fenton was born in 1747. His *A Historical Tour Through Pembrokeshire* was published in 1811.

Godebert the Fleming (1094–1131) was part of the Norman dominion over Pembrokeshire and St Jerome's Church in Llangwm was erected in 1185 under the patronage of his grandson Adam de la Roche, who later built Roch Castle. The name of Roche was acquired from the parish of Roch, within the cantref of Rhos.

Nolton Haven, a short distance south of Newgale, was originally a Welsh settlement – 'old-tun' – appropriated by incomers around the time of the Norman Conquest. From medieval times, it was a small port that exported coal. A tramway later ran from the haven over the hill to Trefrane Colliery.

Today, Nolton is a small, attractive cove considered by many to be dangerous because of strong currents. From its small beach, at low tide, it affords views across the whole of St Brides Bay and the islands.

It was here on Christmas Day 1810 that the *Linen Hall*, sailing from Dublin to the West Indies, ran aground. For once there was no loss of life and it was reported that 'little was taken from the wreck'. The ship was eventually broken up and the timber and rigging sold in the area.

For over fifty years St Brides Bay has been a safe haven to oil tankers from all over the world, as each wait their turn for inward passage to enter the refineries of Milford Haven (Aberdaugleddau) before departing homeward bound. On looking out to sea, the silhouettes of these huge vessels are so conspicuous. The dichotomy that exists in balancing the economic benefits of the oil industry with a fragile habitat is especially marked off the coast of Pembrokeshire. Today more than ever, there is an acute awareness of the environmental concerns caused by shipping.

The International Maritime Organisation is just one worldwide body responsible for monitoring carbon emissions from container shipping and pollution caused by leaks from oil tankers. This is in addition to the maritime agencies and government departments within the United Kingdom.

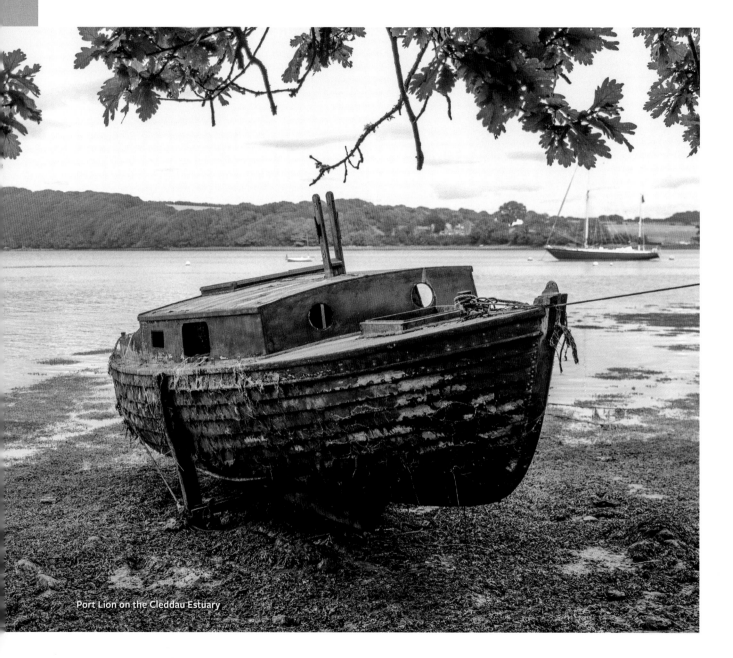

Port Lion on the Cleddau Estuary

Photographing Pembrokeshire | A Paradise for Pirates

Waves regularly crash onto the beaches around St Brides Bay bringing in all manner of flotsam and jetsam. At one time it was mainly driftwood, and occasionally some debris from a passing vessel, that polluted our waters. Today, there is a massive problem with plastic waste, maliciously and selfishly jettisoned from passing vessels far out at sea, choking the oceans, concealed from government control. Since the Government of Canada proposed the concept of a World Ocean Day at the Earth Summit in Rio de Janeiro in 2002, the problem has had a higher profile. In 2008, the United Nations officially recognised 8 June as being World Oceans Day, a specific opportunity to help protect and conserve the shared oceans of the world, essential to the health of future generations.

Sir David Attenborough, in his recent breathtaking production *Blue Planet II*, vividly demonstrated the blight that pollution brings to our environment and that of marine life. There are apparently five trillion pieces of plastic floating in the world's seas. It is now an acknowledged paradox that 'ghost nets' can potentially shed micro plastics that deter fish from returning to traditional fishing grounds, thereby reducing the catch and revenue of those who live off the sea.

Iolo Williams, Welsh naturalist, broadcaster, writer and passionate conservationist, who is a patron of and ambassador for several conservation organisations, also continues to make an immense contribution to protecting wildlife. Wildlife Trusts Wales, the Welsh Ornithological Society and the Sea Trust are but a few of the institutions through which he is attempting to halt the dramatic decline in wildlife and endangered species.

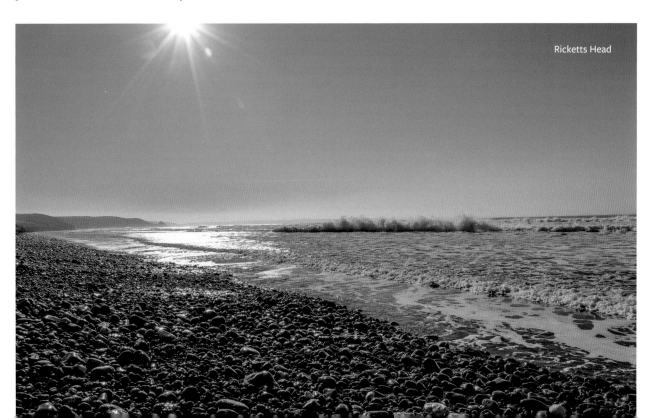

Ricketts Head

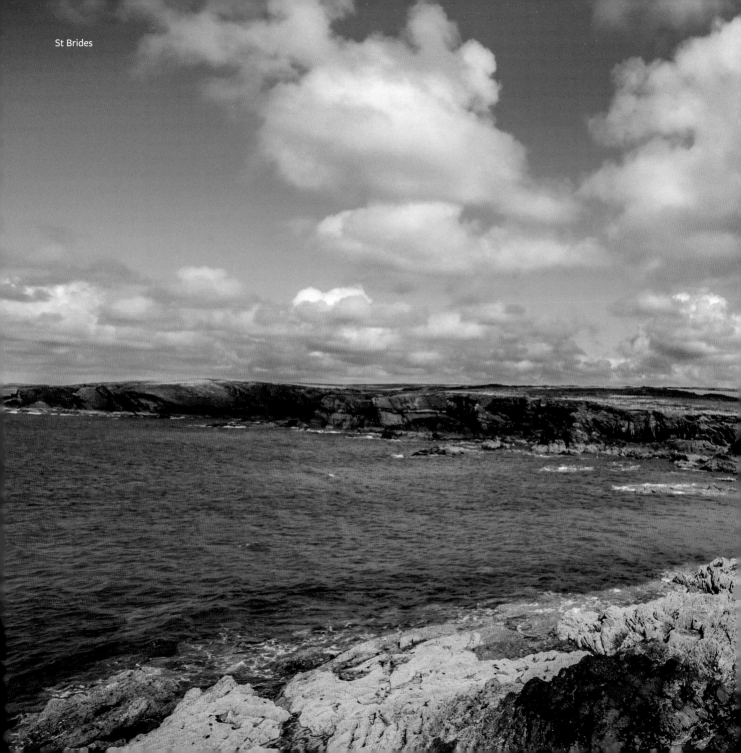

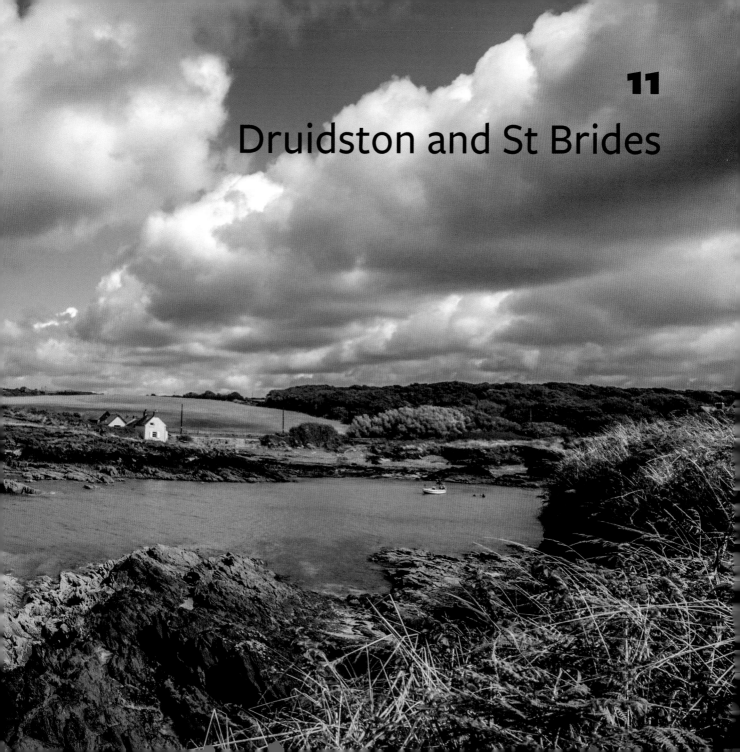

11

Druidston and St Brides

Isolation, confinement and Germanic kindness

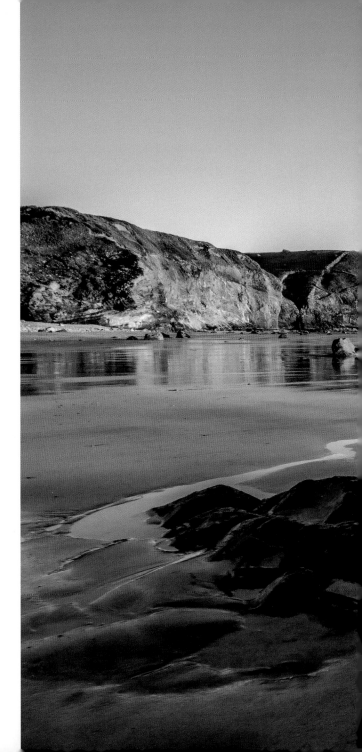

RUIDSTON, NAMED AFTER 'Drue', one of the many Norman knights in the area in the twelfth century, is renowned for its secluded and scenic beach, enclosed by three steeply rising cliffs. It is located in the mouth of St Brides Bay and possesses an atmosphere of hippy quirkiness, harking back to a mid 1960s subculture of psychedelia when California and Swinging London were the centre of the teenage universe – then a long way from Pembrokeshire. It still to this day attracts characters reliving that era, who characteristically arrive in a VW camper van, equipped with acoustic guitar and a headband concealing their receding hair. There is an ambience of complete freedom. In former days, the area was well out of view of prying eyes and was admirably suited for smuggling, and to some extent still is off the beaten track today.

Between 4 and 6 January 1791, the *Increase of Scarborough* a 'merchantman' ship, got into difficulties at Druidston. The 150-ton ship had set sail from the West Indies in the August of the previous year and was carrying a cargo of condemned gunpowder and mounted guns from the British garrison on Saint Kitts. While beached, the ship was plundered for the copper hoops that bound the barrels of gunpowder. A spark, caused by drunken recklessness after consuming the rum on board, set off a chain of three explosions, with fatal consequences.

Between Druidston and St Brides (Sain Ffraid) the coastal path passes the quaint holiday village of Little Haven (Hafan Fach), above which are popular campsites.

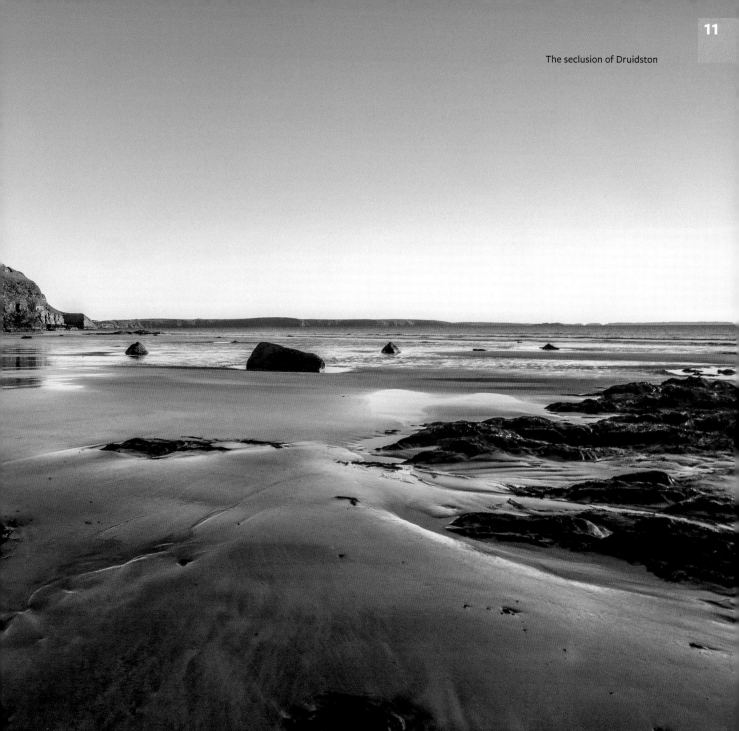

The seclusion of Druidston

St Brides Castle

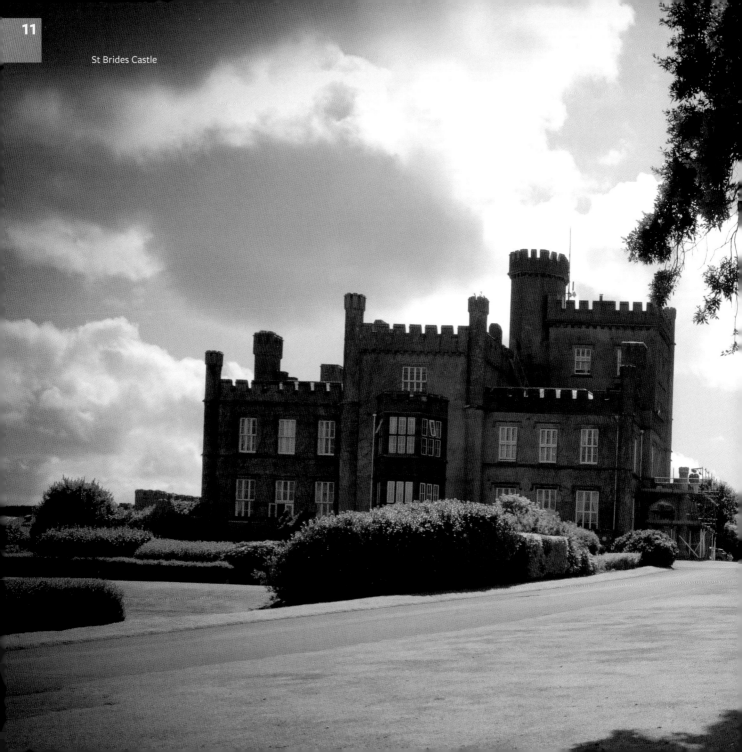

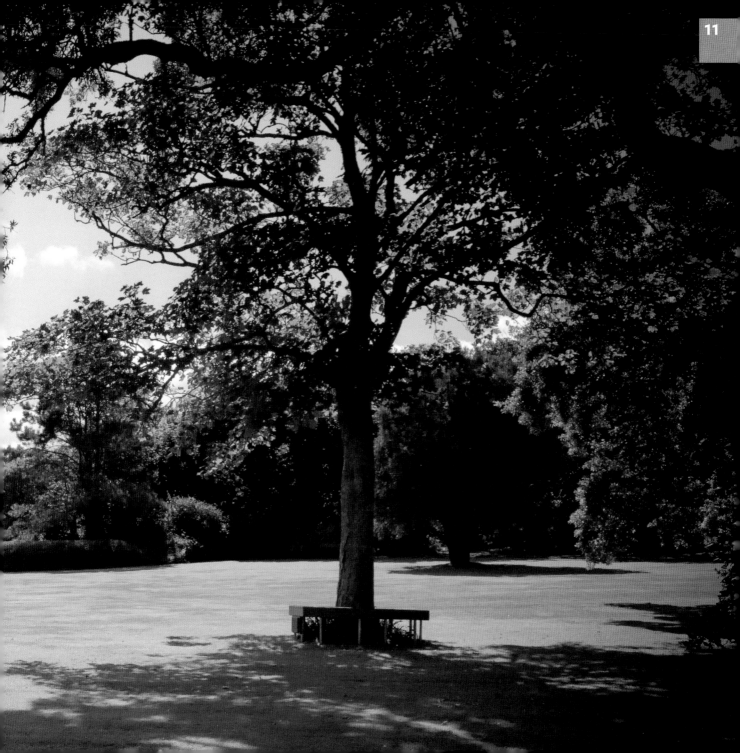

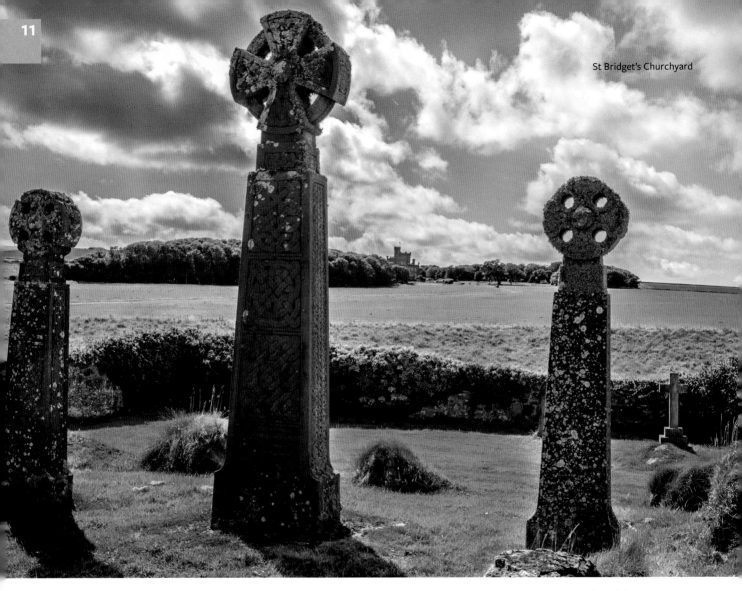

St Bridget's Churchyard

The walk then continues for some distance through deciduous woodland, isolated from the hordes of families that settle on the beach for the day. The beauty and tranquillity of this setting was tragically shattered on 29th June 1989, when local serial killer and prolific criminal John Cooper brutally murdered Peter and Gwenda Dixon from Oxfordshire, who had been camping nearby. Four years earlier, Cooper had gone undetected when he preyed upon another couple seven miles further inland, killing them and burning their farmhouse to the ground.

Welsh director Marc Evans captured the location and related the chilling story sensitively in the television drama *The Pembrokeshire Murders*. The serial showed the determination of DS Steve Wilkins of Dyfed Powys Police, who eventually managed to secure Cooper's conviction.

The serene inlet of St Brides and the imposing St Brides Castle reveal a diverse history, coupled with a series of most unlikely visitations during the first half of the twentieth century. The cove itself is currently used as dive site and attracts many from all over Britain interested in marine life and adventure. Such educational opportunities, coupled with a sensitive awareness of environmental issues, were not at the forefront of the mind of a visitor to the area in the 1920s.

The castle, set in 99 acres of mature parkland, was the former country residence of Lord and Lady Kensington. In 1923 their home was sold to the King Edward VII Welsh National Memorial Association in order that it could be opened as Kensington Hospital. Between 1923 and 1978 it served as a TB isolation hospital. Before the availability of antibiotics such as penicillin in the 1940s and further research into the dreaded disease of tuberculosis, the long road to recovery in those dark years involved fresh air and plenty of rest at sanatoriums such as this. Visitors came to St Brides during those gloomy days perhaps with little choice, and for no reason other than to seek isolation in an attempt to contain what was then the killer disease known as consumption.

The period immediately after the Second World War brought another type of visitor, again with little choice, but who certainly made a significant contribution and lit up the lives of those who were bedridden at this hospital. In 1946, German prisoners of war from Rommel's Afrika Corps, based at the POW camp at Portfield, Haverfordwest, worked in the grounds of Kensington Hospital and are today remembered by former patients for their kindness in bringing fresh fruits from the hospital gardens to the children on the wards, and making their period of isolation both interesting and comfortable. On 16 May 2009, a commemorative plaque was unveiled in the grounds of St Brides Castle, during a moving ceremony that recognised patient care at the sanatorium.

There were, however, episodes of happiness as a result of German internment. July 1947 was the occasion of the first wedding in Britain between a German POW and a British woman. Hans Pilawa, a prisoner at the Portfield Camp, and Mary Owen, a local woman who worked for the Pembrokeshire War Agricultural Committee, were permitted to marry in the local Registry Office, although their wedding night was not very traditional: Hans had to return to the camp and was only allowed to phone Mary to wish her goodnight.

Repatriation of German prisoners of war took a long time and only began in late 1947. Some chose to stay, usually because they had fallen in love with local women. Several are still in Pembrokeshire, having made the county their home for seventy years. They are respected as hard workers who have contributed to life in the county.

Today the whole of the former Kensington Hospital is luxury holiday apartments. Little did young children think during their long periods of confinement in the 1940s that in the following century, visitors to the county would be investing in a holiday property bond, in order to share the same uninterrupted view of St Brides Bay they once had.

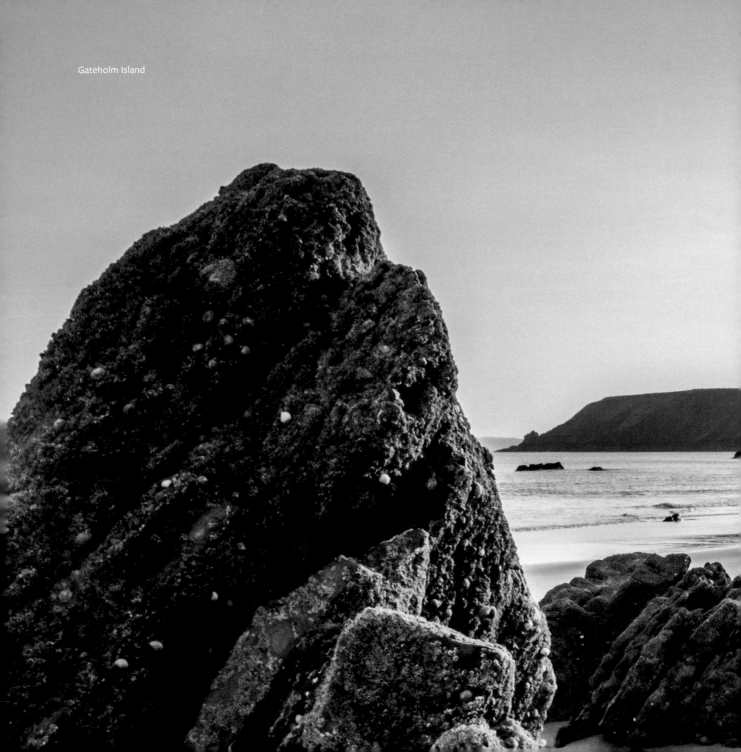

Gateholm Island

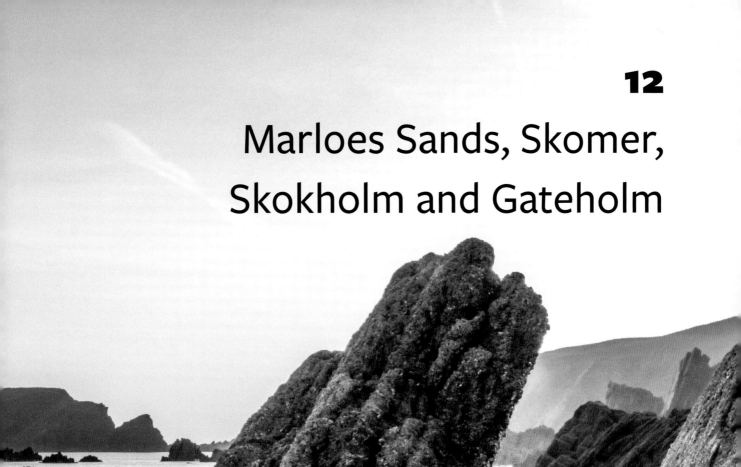

12

Marloes Sands, Skomer, Skokholm and Gateholm

The invasion of the protected islands

THE PEACEFUL BEACH at Marloes with its wonderful rock formation, far away from public gaze, is 'within touching distance' of the islands of Skomer, Skokholm and Gateholm. These islands, named by inquisitive Vikings, were once used by pirates to store plunder, and are now protected bird sanctuaries.

Skomer – Ynys Sgomer in Welsh, coming from *Skalmey*, of Viking origin, meanin=g 'Cleft Island' – is a National Nature Reserve, a Site of Special Scientific Interest and a Special Protection Area. It was once the home of the Codd family, before being bought for the nation in 1959.

Today, thousands of bird watchers, wildlife enthusiasts and photographers travel from all over the world in order to access the islands from Martins Haven. Visitors come to the islands to observe the Atlantic puffin, the Manx shearwater, the razorbill, the Skomer vole and a whole host of other wildlife that settle here at certain times of the year. Wildlife photographers worldwide make the journey equipped with telephoto lenses and an array of equipment, to spend hours dwelling upon the quaint characteristics of the puffin and to capture the iconic image with sand eels in its beak.

Due to the uncanny noises of the furtive Manx shearwater during the night, the Vikings nicknamed Skomer 'Ghost Island'. The Manx shearwaters travel all the way from South America to invade the islands to raise their young.

In 1927, Ronald Lockley and his wife Doris took a 21-year lease on the uninhabited island of Skokholm (Ynys Sgogwm in Welsh, coming from the Norse for 'Wooded Island') in order to study wildlife and to observe the migratory habits of birds they encountered on the island.

Film directors have been attracted to the unique beauty of this area and have on occasions descended with cast and crew to invade its relaxed environment. Such sorties have promoted tourism and enhanced the economy. Film director Anthony Harvey used the setting of Marloes Sands as the backdrop for the 1968 Academy Award-winning film *The Lion in Winter*. The location was again chosen for another award-winning film released in 2012, *Snow White and the Huntsman*.

Gateholm Island (Old Norse for 'Goat Island'), a small tidal island on the southwest tip of the county, lies between Marloes Sands and the two islands and was formerly a Roman settlement. Located here is the treacherous shortcut known to mariners as Jack Sound, where many a vessel has foundered. In April 1837, the paddle steamer *Albion* came to grief with her crew, passengers and cargo. At Albion Sands at low tide, machinery that once belonged to the vessel is still visible. On 16 January 1865, the schooner *Cordella*, sailing from Penzance, Cornwall and laden with coal, ran aground at Marloes Sands. The vessel lay on its beam end until its cargo was washed out, after which it was salvaged. There was no plundering on this occasion.

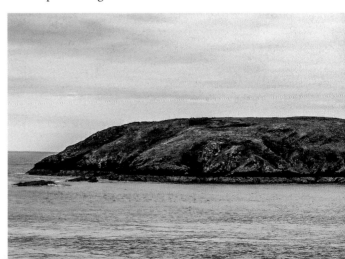

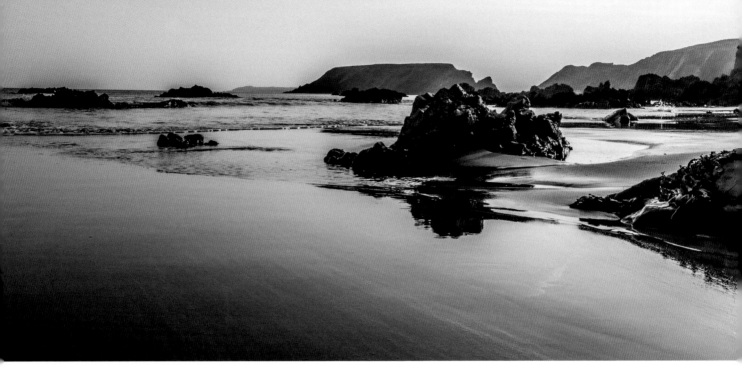

Marloes Sands

The Deer Park, located on the tip of the Marloes peninsula, is managed by the National Trust and affords magnificent views over the islands and St Brides Bay. Inhabited by wild ponies and Welsh Black calves that graze there, its name is a misnomer – no deer have ever lived there!

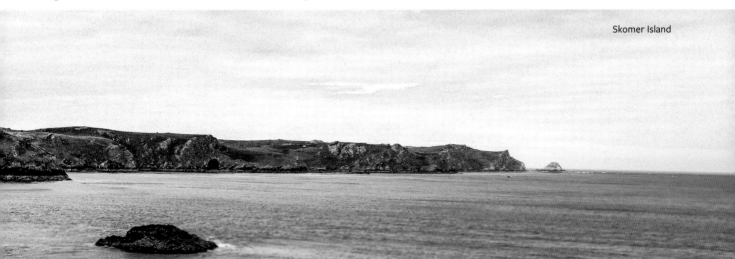

Skomer Island

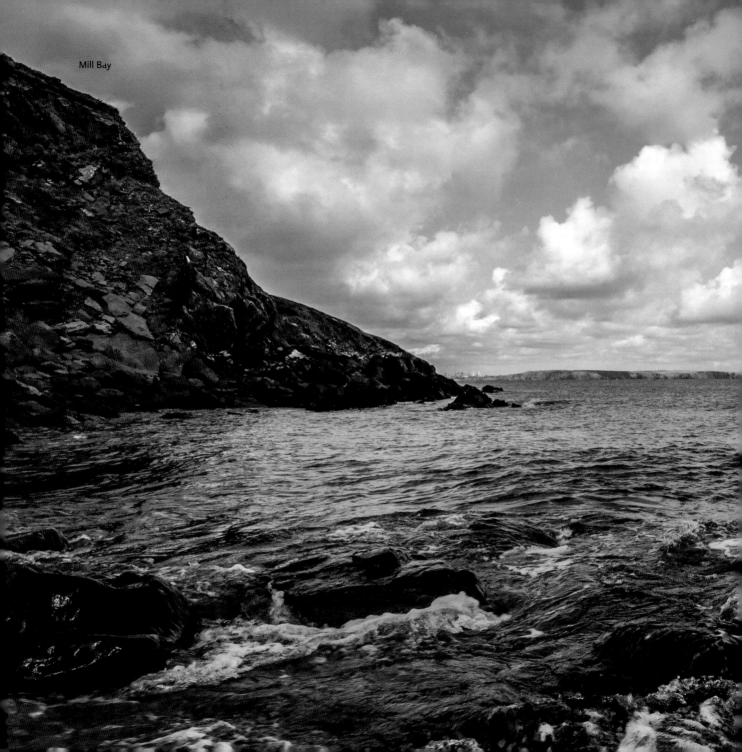

Mill Bay

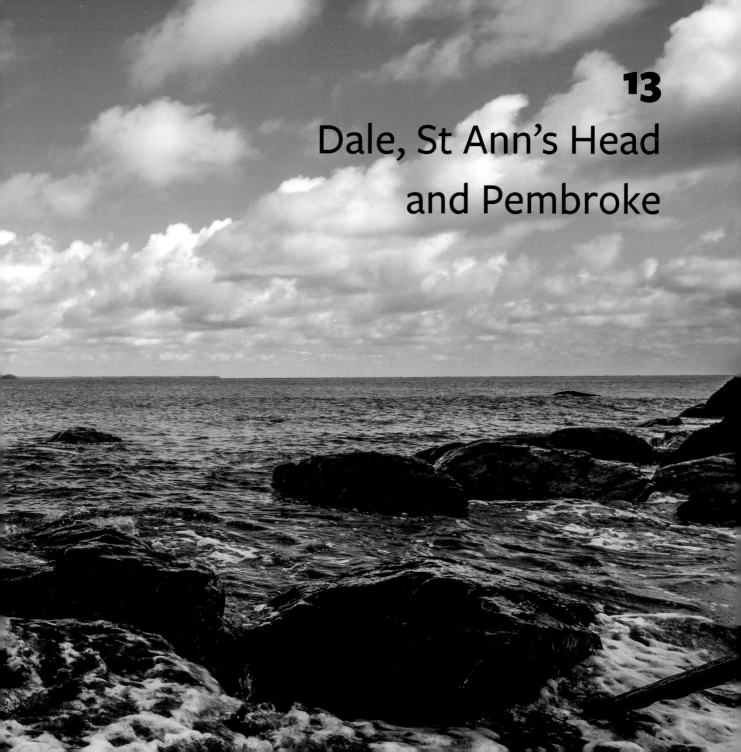

13

Dale, St Ann's Head and Pembroke

The birth of the Tudor dynasty and the Civil War in Wales

DURING THE FIFTEENTH century, the area around Dale witnessed an absurd paradox: an 'invasion' by a Welshman, Henry Tudor, whose purpose was to claim the Crown of England. Having been born in Pembroke Castle in 1457, the 28 year old, who had but a tenuous claim to the throne, entered 'through the back door' when he sailed from France, where he had been sheltered by his uncle, Jasper. He landed in the area between St Ann's Head and Dale, known as Mill Bay, with 55 ships and 4,000 men, before making his march to Bosworth Field, where he defeated Richard III on 22 August 1485.

The Tudor dynasty was thereby established. This fulfilled the ancient Welsh prophecy that the Welsh would regain Britain from the Saxons, since Henry was not only Welsh-born but also directly descended on his father's side from Rhys ap Gruffydd – 'the Lord Rhys', one of the most powerful of Welsh princes. The consequence of this victory, however, was seen by some to be the suppression of the Welsh language, culture and identity. Though it saw the ascendancy of the Welsh gentry classes holding public office and court in England, Wales was to become an English colony, particularly during the subsequent reign of Henry VIII.

Pembroke Castle, built between 1190 and 1245, dominates the town, being strategically placed at the hub of the Anglo-Norman colony. It is ranked as the most powerful Norman fortress in the Principality. It was to be particularly prominent again almost 200 years after

Henry Tudor seized the crown at Bosworth, when John Poyer, Rowland Laugharne and Rice Powell, who had strong links with the South Pembrokeshire gentry, led an insurgence that caused Oliver Cromwell to invade across the border to crush their revolt. During the period when the English Civil War was reaching its close, the three Parliamentarians changed sides and led a Royalist uprising in 1648, disgruntled over arrears of army pay owed to them for services rendered. They retreated west and were ultimately forced to take refuge within the precincts of the castle. Oliver Cromwell, himself of Welsh ancestry (his great-grandfather was Richard Williams), personally took it upon himself to take control of the situation and rode to Pembroke (Penfro) with a Parliamentary force, but only took the castle after a seven-week siege. The castle, which stands on a rocky promontory surrounded on three sides by the Cleddau Estuary, proved to be insurmountable, and only surrendered when the conduit pipe providing the water supply was cut off.

The castle featured in a 1989 BBC production of *The Chronicles of Narnia* by C S Lewis.

This corner of Pembrokeshire opens out to the Atlantic Ocean and the Celtic Sea and, in consequence, experiences tempestuous winds and storms through which many a ship has met its end. St Ann's Head and its imposing lighthouse fittingly guard the entrance to the Milford Haven (Aberdaugleddau) waterway.

The coastal stretch from Cardiff (Caerdydd) to Milford Haven has also seen a proliferation of wrecking and smuggling, plunderers preying on everyday commodities being shuttled to and from the tiny ports along the coast. The local gentry, outwardly law abiding or an integral part of the criminal justice system, often sponsored the reprehensible activities of those plunderers. On 2 September 1757, the French ship *La Muette*, sailing from

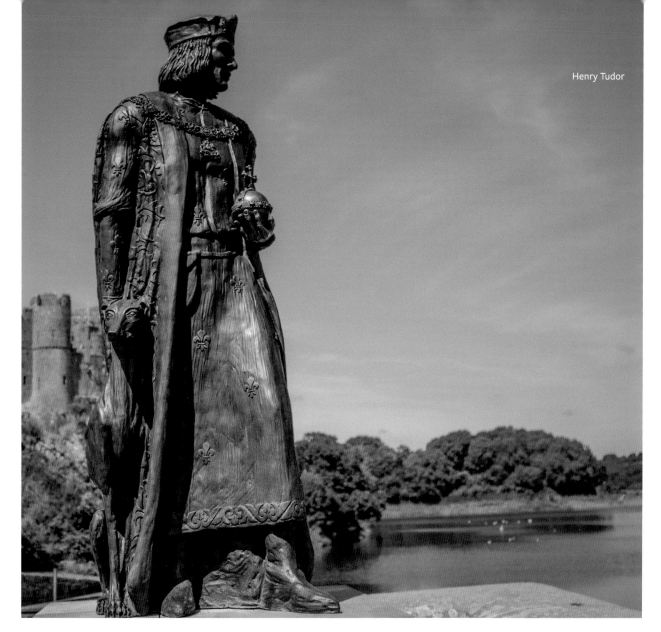

Henry Tudor

Bordeaux to Canada laden with wine, baled goods and small arms, was forced to shelter and ran aground near Dale. On breaking up, its valuable cargo mysteriously vanished into the surrounding area.

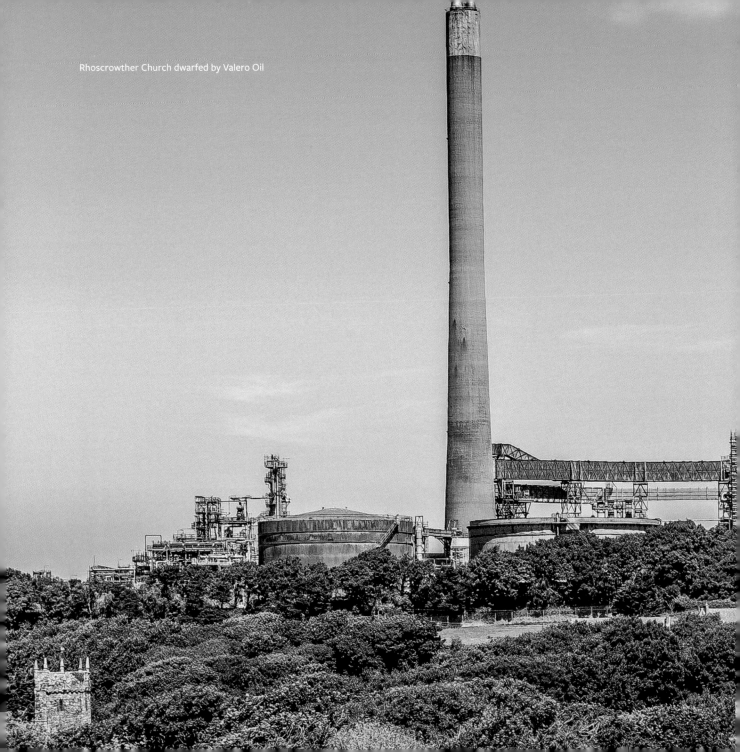

Rhoscrowther Church dwarfed by Valero Oil

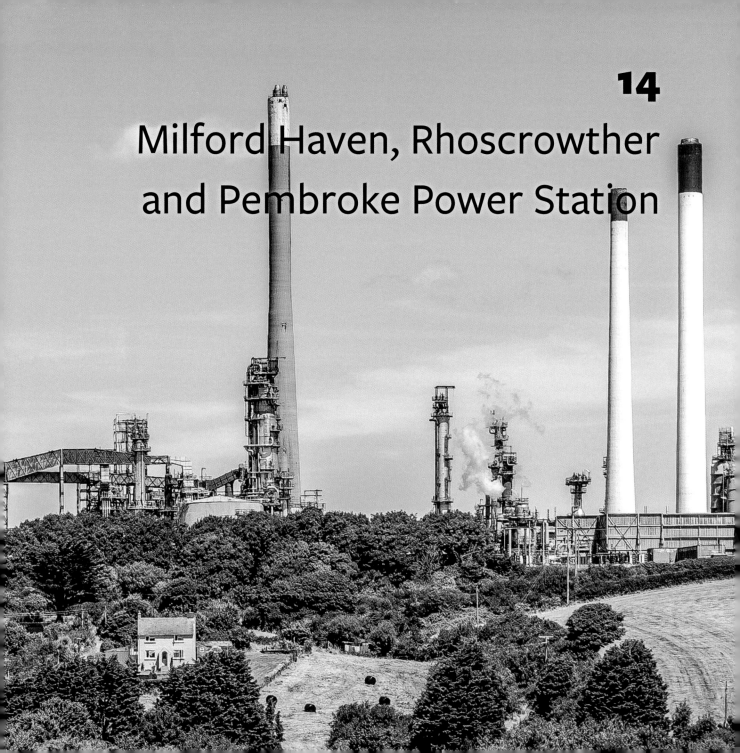

14

Milford Haven, Rhoscrowther and Pembroke Power Station

Nantucket whalers, Quakers, the perpetual threat from France and Spain and the *Sea Empress* disaster

MILFORD HAVEN (ABERDAUGLEDDAU) developed quite late in the eighteenth century, having earlier experienced both invasion and migration for secular and religious reasons. Before its development as a port, it was used as a base for forces to shelter and as a staging post from which to invade Ireland. During the ninth century, Milford Haven and its surrounding area were targeted by Viking raiders, with Norse Chieftain Hubba (from whom Hubberston gets its name) being prominent amongst them. There were subsequent Norman invasions and later the area saw the emergence of Hywel Davies (*c.*1690–1719), who became known as the 'Cavalier Prince of Pirates'. Though he based his piratical activities in the Caribbean and the Gold Coast (West Africa) he was responsible for introducing Pembrokeshire-born Bartholomew Roberts – Barti Ddu – to the high seas and was thereafter surpassed by him in many respects.

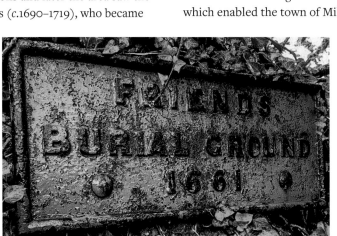

Burial ground at Sutton East Hook

Prior to the establishment of Milford Haven as a port in 1793, the area had a strong religious community, which was to play a significant part in its development. In 1682, many members of the Religious Society of Friends (Quakers) who had lived in the county migrated overseas to the colony of Pennsylvania, founded by William Penn, in order to escape persecution. The passing of the Toleration Act in 1689, however, allowed freedom of worship for Nonconformist religious groups, and Pembrokeshire saw the return of some Quaker whalers. Sir William Hamilton, a British diplomat and politician who through marriage owned the land in the area, together with his nephew Sir Charles Greville approached three leading whaler merchants and several Quaker families from Nantucket and Martha's Vineyard, Massachusetts to settle in the town and to form a whaling fleet. This proved attractive as it coincided with the end of the American War of Independence in 1783, and their strong desire to relocate their business across the Atlantic. Hamilton steered legislation through Parliament in 1790 which enabled the town of Milford Haven, its docks and quays to be built, with one of the deepest natural harbours in the world.

In 1811 the Quaker Meeting House was built on a site acquired in 1801 for a burial ground. A Friends' Burial Ground had been earlier established some six miles away from Milford Haven, at East Hook. The establishment of a 'Friends' Meeting House' founded by settlers from America who were the descendants of those who had emigrated from Britain was indeed unique. The Welsh poet, Waldo Williams worshipped here, after becoming a Quaker in his mid fifties.

The town of Milford Haven was designed on a grid system similar to Boston, Massachusetts and has place names linked with Nantucket and the early settlers who arrived there. Ship's captain Zacchary Bunker and Uriah Bunker (Bunkers' Hill) and Samuel Starbuck (Starbuck Road) are well-known names in the area, as well as Nantucket Avenue. Connections continue in the world of the arts: in the 1851 novel *Moby Dick* by Herman Melville, the chief mate of the whaler *Pequod* is named Starbuck and is a Quaker from Nantucket. In the film version, shot off Fishguard, he is played by Leo Genn.

When Nelson visited in 1802 as part of a tour to celebrate the anniversary of the Battle of the Nile, he commented that Milford Haven was one of the two finest natural harbours he had ever seen. It was no coincidence that Sir William Hamilton's second wife Emma Hamilton had links to Horatio Nelson. During the Napoleonic Wars, Milford Haven became a Royal Navy Dockyard, until it was relocated to Pembroke Dock (Doc Penfro) in 1814.

Milford Haven was of strategic importance and by the late 1850s there was growing concern over the build-up of the military and naval power of France and the ability of the United Kingdom to defend itself against invasion. The Royal Commission on the Defence of the United Kingdom, reporting in 1860, consequently recommended that a series of forts be built around the entrance to Pembroke Dock and Milford Haven. The projected cost for Pembrokeshire alone was £765,000. They were built in polygonal style around key areas at the mouth of the Haven, and radically changed the face of the county. They still remain a curiosity and are of historical interest.

Thorn Island, at West Angle Bay, has a magnificent vista over the entrance to the Haven and was at one stage converted into hotel accommodation. Stack Rock Fort, offshore at Milford Haven, was once heavily fortified with turret guns and a garrison of nearly 200 soldiers. Today it nestles beneath the original Esso Oil Refinery with the attractive backdrop of the Preseli Hills (Mynyddoedd y Preseli). Popton Fort, overlooking Angle Bay, is housed on private land owned by the Valero Oil Refinery. The area is very security conscious and is out of bounds to any photographer. Hubberston Fort is another that is strategically placed on the Haven at Gelliswick Bay, today flanked by oil installations. St Catherine's Fort, a tidal island further south linked to Tenby (Dinbych-y-pysgod)'s South Beach, remains iconic and has been used for all manner of enterprises. In 2016, the BBC TV series *Sherlock* filmed on location in Pembrokeshire, portraying it as a maximum-security prison.

These defences became known as 'Palmerston Forts', promoted by the then Prime Minister, Lord Palmerston. They were later considered to be worthless strategically, as by the 1880s the threat from France had long since dissipated. 'Palmerston's Follies' were rated extravagant, needless structures erected at a time when Britain was at peace with France.

On 27 September 1888, the first steam trawler entered Milford Haven's newly opened dock. It was the *Sybil*, registered in Lowestoft. Thereafter, Belgian, Dutch and Spanish skippers would come ashore and socialise in pubs and clubs that they came to regard as 'their local'. The residents regarded each day as a pay day as the fishermen spent their hard-earned cash in the community. The port of Milford Haven remains the largest fishing port in Wales. It was to become a cosmopolitan melting pot when nationalities from all over Western Europe docked here.

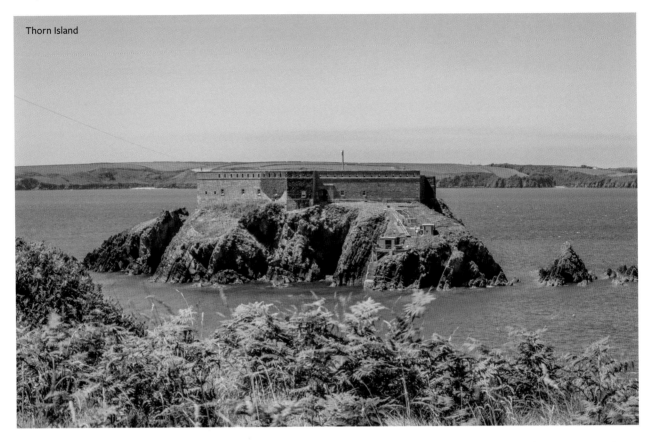

Thorn Island

Its hinterland, which is way down below the Landsker, is very much an English-speaking community.

The late 1950s saw yet another development; this on an unprecedented scale and eagerly greeted by many as the key to boosting local employment, but that enthusiasm was predictably short-lived. This was the construction of major oil installations around the Milford Haven Waterway (Dyfrffordd Aberdaugleddau). In 1960 the Esso oil refinery was opened in Milford Haven, soon followed by BP, Texaco, Gulf and in 1971, Amoco. In some instances

the effect upon the environment was devastating, raising acute concerns over health and safety. For the inhabitants of the medieval village of Rhoscrowther (Rhoscrowdder), which once nestled in the pretty valley south of the Texaco installation, in the community of Hundleton, their whole way of life was to be radically changed when as a result of thirty years of tolerating the acrid smells of sulphur and toxic pollution, there was an offer to buy the village. Chevron and its successor, Valero, one of the largest oil refineries in Europe, may well have

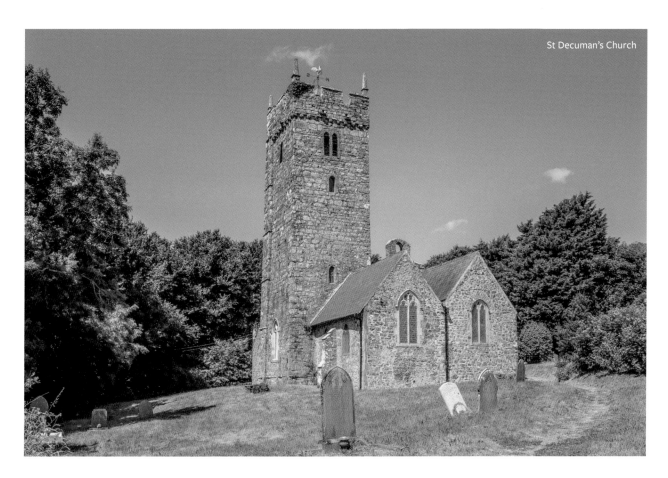

St Decuman's Church

brought employment to the area but at a significant cost to others. Today, what remains around the Valero Oil Refinery is an abandoned village and the Church of St Decuman Grade I listed and carefully maintained by the Friends of Friendless Churches charity, together with the neighbouring Schoolhouse. The stacks and paraphernalia of the domineering oil refinery dwarf the village.

In 2011 four contractors were killed and a fifth suffered life-changing burns when flammable gases ignited inside a chemical storage tank at the then Chevron refinery, caused by health and safety breaches. In 2019, at Swansea Crown Court, Chevron was fined £5 million and ordered to pay £1 million costs. In addition, specialist cleaning company B & A Contracts was heavily fined and penalised in costs for systematic failings. Health and Safety Executive Officer Andrew Knowles said that the accident "was entirely preventable, with numerous opportunities missed to save workers' lives".

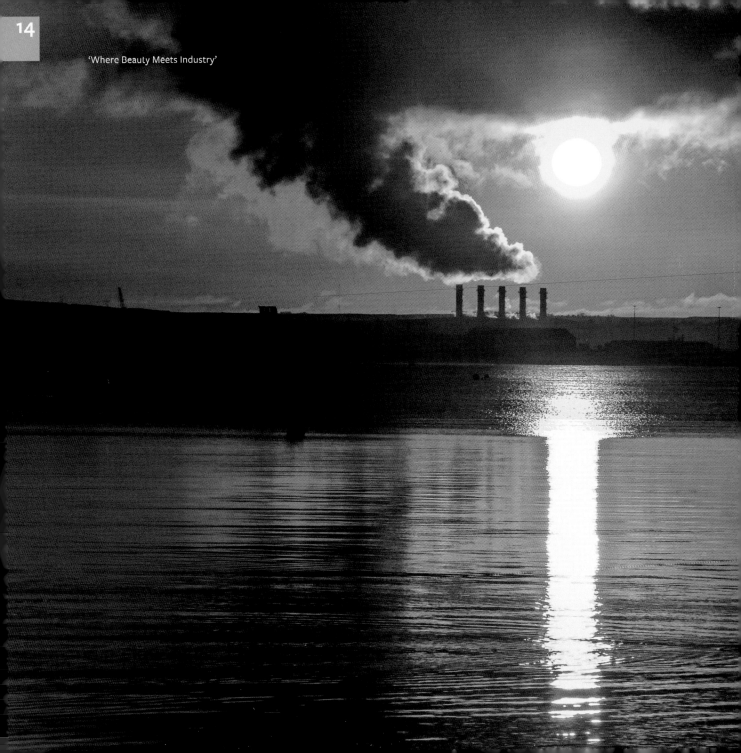

'Where Beauty Meets Industry'

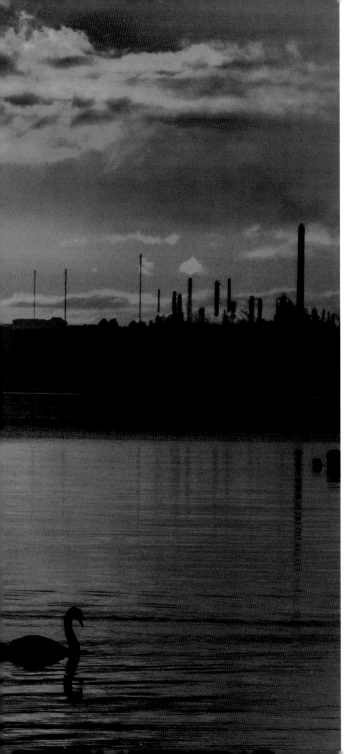

In October 2016, the Valero Oil Company were castigated as being arrogant over their failure to deal adequately with a spillage of some 140,000 litres of oil into the Nant Pibiwr river, caused by a fractured pipeline carrying aviation fuel and diesel under the A48 at Nantycaws, Carmarthenshire (Sir Gâr). As recently as January 2019, another spillage of oil occurred on the south side of the estuary at Sandy Haven. Though less significant in quantity, it once more raised obvious concerns about environmental protection. This demonstrates the inherent dangers associated with unbridled development and its insidious effect within the county. In September 2019, climate change activists set up a one-day blockade and peaceful protest outside the entrance to the refinery, causing significant disruption to the site.

Between 2015 and 2018, Rhoscrowther Wind Farm Ltd. submitted three unsuccessful proposals for the installation of five 100-metre tall wind turbines to be built within the Haven Waterway Enterprise Zone. All three were refused as it was ruled that 'this development would have a significant and adverse visual effect on the character and appearance of the landscape of the Pembrokeshire Coast National Park. It was ruled that 'the harm caused would outweigh the benefits it would bring' and that 'it would cause substantial damage to the setting of St Decumanus, its cross and schoolhouse'.

The impact of implementing such development within the Pembrokeshire Coast National Park in the twenty-first century was the deciding factor, despite the overwhelming decision fifty years earlier to permit the conspicuous scarring of the coast and skyline through the invasive presence of the major oil companies and the industrialisation of the Milford Haven Waterway. This striking inconsistency on the part of Pembrokeshire County Council defies common sense and remains an uncomfortable contradiction.

Chemical and crude oil tankers sailing under flags from all over the world enter the haven with their vast tonnage, 'invading' on a daily basis from the Middle East and the Gulf, docking in Pembroke and exploiting the advantages that the natural deep water harbour of Milford Haven has to offer. Though the Esso Oil Refinery and Marine Terminal was closed around 1980 and dismantled in 1983, the South Hook liquefied natural gas (LNG) terminal and storage facility was built on the former site in 2006, with a second terminal at Waterston. LNG is shipped around the world by tanker, treated and converted to its natural state at these terminals and pumped via a massive pipeline to the gas network in Britain.

Observing a chemical/oil tanker sailing in St Brides Bay (Bae Sain Ffraid) under the flag of, say, the Marshall Islands with an overall length of 315 m, a beam of 50 m and a gross tonnage of 136,000 alongside a yacht with an overall length of just 10 m with a lonely mariner at the helm is quite bizarre, but is in fact, a commonplace sight. At night, it is common to see an armada of illuminated tankers in St Brides Bay, against a backdrop of the flaming stacks of the oil refineries at Milford Haven and the plume of smoke billowing from Pembroke Power Station. This is the largest gas-fired power station in Europe, where beauty meets industry on a level apparently acceptable in the Pembrokeshire National Park: a dichotomy that remains controversial in the eyes of many. Whether this incursion is part of a rich melting pot or a serious blight on natural beauty is open to debate.

On Thursday, 15 February 1996, this Vegas-like illuminated image of the coastline was totally destroyed by an oil spill on an unprecedented scale. The *Sea Empress*, an oil tanker registered in Monrovia, Liberia and weighing 147,273 tonnes with a crew of 27, ran aground at 20:07 hours on rocks at St Ann's Head at the entrance to Milford Haven Waterway en route to the Texaco oil refinery. The impact upon the environment and clean-up operation was colossal. This disaster was very close to the national nature reserve islands of Skomer and Skokholm. The wildlife on those protected islands was devastated when 72,000 tonnes of crude oil saturated 125 miles of coastline in one of Europe's most important and sensitive wildlife and marine conservation areas. At a cost of £60 million and the commitment of Pembrokeshire Council, Texaco workers and wildlife conservationists working assiduously over a period of about five years, the marine wildlife population was more or less returned to normal and the coastline was restored almost to its former self.

The 1980s witnessed piratical activities of a fashion when Spanish-owned, British-registered vessels based in Milford Haven demonstrated staggering arrogance in overfishing the waters off Ireland and to the west of Scotland. Their catch would be landed in the ports of northern Spain, netting them millions of pounds through pure dishonesty. Their fraudulent conduct extended to under-declaration of their actual catch, falsifying logbooks, and failure to record the species of fish caught. The *Whitesands* was one of a fleet of such pirate vessels, whose skipper was eventually convicted at Swansea Crown Court and received a substantial penalty on several counts of fraud, alongside a record fine for the company that owned the boat.

In 1993, Welsh fishermen were so outraged over the actions of the Government in giving way to French fishing quotas in Brussels, and increasingly annoyed by the way that the port of Milford Haven had become a French fishing colony, that they took direct steps to prevent what in their eyes were acts of piracy in home waters. They prevented the Milford-based French trawler the *Jane de Lorraine* – carrying 40 tons of fish – from entering the

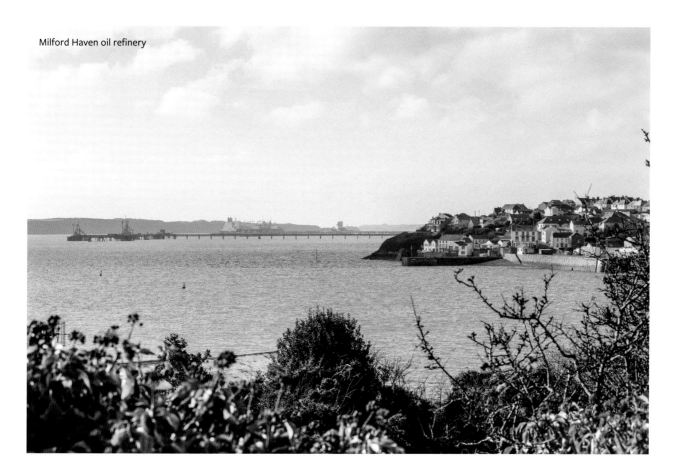

Milford Haven oil refinery

harbour and forced it to anchor on the Cleddau Estuary. A further three French vessels were held inside the port of Milford Haven before the blockade was eventually lifted over eight hours later. There was again a heavy police presence at the dockside when local fishermen entered the harbour market and upturned fish that had been boxed by French trawlermen.

Whilst some local fishermen ensure that local restaurants are supplied with a fresh catch on a daily basis, while others quite understandably take their lobster and crab to meet container trucks that regularly arrive at port, to be quietly conveyed to the bistros of Brittany and Normandy. The average Francophile enjoying a glass of Muscadet whilst on holiday on the coast of Northern France frequently overlooks the fact that the seafood it complements is often sourced in Pembrokeshire.

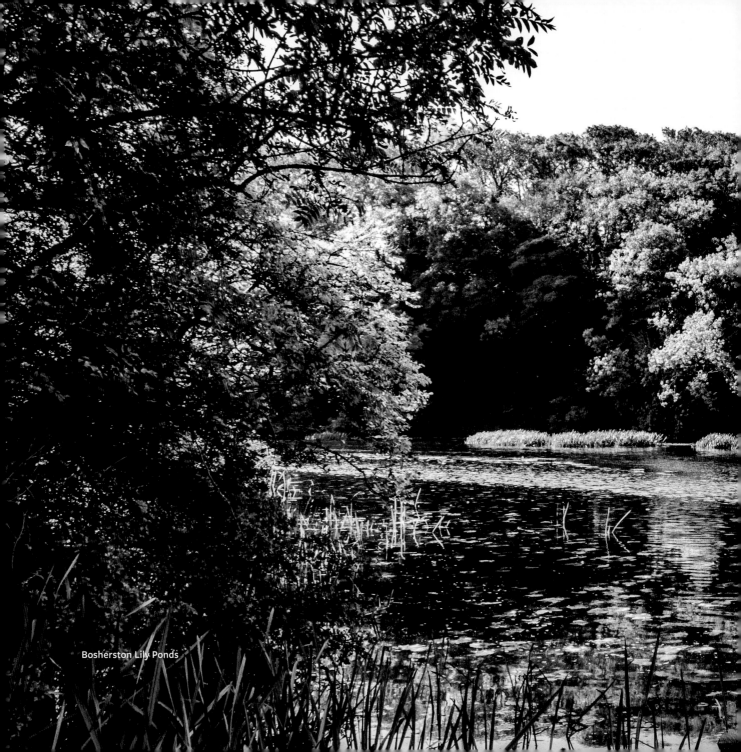

Bosherston Lily Ponds

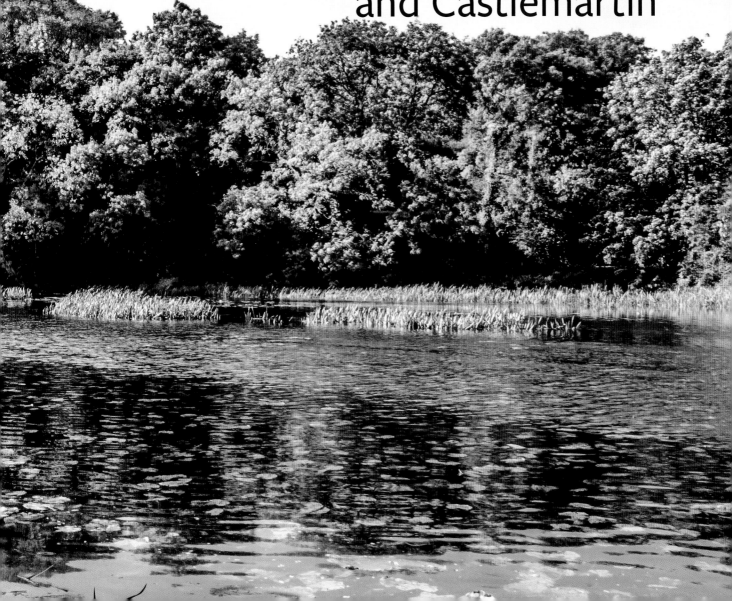

West Angle Bay, Freshwater West and Castlemartin

Utopia and the German invasion

IN THE SIXTEENTH century this area was a busy shipping lane, plagued by acts of piracy and smuggling. Owing to prevailing westerly winds, there were a number of shipwrecks when vessels in transit would come to grief on dangerous rocks, ironically while seeking a safe haven.

The coastal waters around Pembrokeshire (Sir Benfro) gave shelter to yet another pirate during this period. John Callice – born, it is thought, in Tintern, Monmouthshire (Tyndyrn, Sir Fynwy), and enlisted in the Navy around 1571 – was considered one of the most dangerous pirates in the realm. The Admiralty regarded Callice as 'a notorious (pyrate) haunting the coasts of Wales', who escaped detection due to his links to the gentry classes, including people such as Sir John Perrot, Commissioner for Piracy in Pembrokeshire. Callice made his headquarters at the Point House, Angle, then owned by George Clerk. Clerk himself amassed substantial profits from dealing in contraband but was never detected, as he was by coincidence the Customs Officer for the Port of Pembroke (Penfro). The activities of Callice were eventually discovered, and by 1576 he was arrested and imprisoned in the infamous Marshalsea in London. In order to commute his prison sentence he is reputed to have become an informant, exposing the unsavoury links that existed between certain highly respected members of the community and piracy. The precise details of his demise are uncertain, but by 1587 he had either been hanged in Newport (Casnewydd) or killed off the Barbary Coast of North Africa.

On 31 January 1808, a storm forced HMS *Leda*, a 'Man of War' carrying 38 guns, to seek shelter under the cliffs at West Angle Bay, but she was wrecked after the pilot set an incorrect course after mistaking Thorn Island for Stack Rocks due to poor visibility. On 30 January 1894 the *Loch Shiel*, a full-rigged sailing ship built of iron, sailing from Glasgow to Melbourne and Adelaide and carrying – amongst other cargo – cases of whisky, was forced into the Haven near Thorn Rock during a fierce storm. Thorn Island is conspicuous as one of the Palmerston Forts that dominate the entrance to the port of Milford Haven (Aberdaugleddau) – built in 1854 and designed to avert any military threat, the fortress was not placed to assist shipping. At the inquiry it was testified that the ship's Master had decided when in the vicinity of the Smalls to take shelter in the Haven, and that the ship had run into rocks at the south entrance to Milford Haven. Luckily the lifeboat from Angle Point Station had managed to rescue many of the crew and passengers. The inquiry ruled, however, that the *Loch Shiel* 'was not navigated with proper and seaman-like care' when negotiating Thorn Rock, but taking into account his good character and his experience, the Master's certificate of competency was suspended for three months only. Wreckage from the ship came ashore on the nearby beaches. Customs officials, though acting promptly, only recovered sixty cases of whisky, as many more had already disappeared and bottles had been concealed in attics, alcoves or even buried in the sand dunes at Freshwater West.

The coast borders the village of West Angle. Here the general appearance of buildings and their layout is rather quirky. Some of the architecture on the main street is eye-catching, if not idiosyncratic, due to its diverse appearance. This is in marked contrast to the general design of buildings in Pembrokeshire and unlike

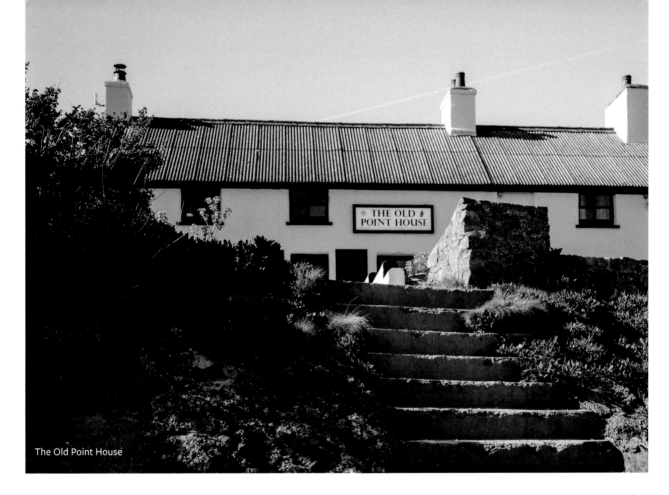

The Old Point House

the traditional concrete-washed roofs that appear on cottages north of the Landsker (which some might call equally peculiar!). On the south side of the main street appears the Globe Hotel, constructed in 1904 from two cottages. This is a three-storey structure with magnificent parapets and crenellations, supported by six cast-iron columns under which the pavement runs. Importing a colonial style of architecture, with a flat roof and sheltered pavement, into a Welsh village was doubtless favoured by the Squire of Angle (Angl), Colonel R W B Mirehouse (1849–1914), who had served in South Africa in 1900 and who was obviously influenced by his experiences outside the county.

After leaving a skyline of oil refineries and power installations, Freshwater West represents coastal beauty on a breathtaking scale – Utopia to some. This is where the Welsh National Surfing Championships are held and surfers visit frequently, making a journey from afar seeking exhilaration and pleasure from the waves. They are very much a discreet type of visitor. Their general appearance and the boards they carry spark memories of nostalgic Beach Boys tracks from iconic vinyl.

The area is renowned for a local delicacy, laver bread, collected from the abundant rocky outcrops prevalent here. In the late 1970s the National Park Authority, with the assistance of a local volunteer group, restored the last thatched seaweed-drying hut in Pembrokeshire, which had been situated on a grassy bank above the beach.

In 1943, during a fierce storm just off the coast, two landing craft that were rehearsing for the Allied landings in Sicily were lost, with 79 soldiers on board and a further six crew from another ship that had come to their rescue.

The area has proved a big hit with film directors and location managers. In 2009, scenes from *Harry Potter and the Deathly Hallows* Parts 1 and 2 set near Shell House were filmed on the beach at Freshwater West. Immediately afterwards, film director Ridley Scott used the location for the production of *Robin Hood* with Russell Crowe and Cate Blanchett. Christopher Nolan, director of the epic 2017 film *Dunkirk*, considered the beach as a location before opting for Dorset. The descent upon a small, cordial county by people not seeking to dominate or intrude upon the lifestyle of an insular community is most welcome. In addition to the understandable excitement of witnessing or being part of the action, it promotes the economy as well as the tourist trade.

The utopian pleasures of Freshwater West are, however, abruptly halted when coastal walkers leave the golden sands to make their way towards the village of Castlemartin (Castell Martin). Castlemartin is situated on the site of a Norman motte-and-bailey castle and had a church dedicated to St Martin, the French Bishop of Tours, hence the name. The village has been English speaking for over 900 years. Castlemartin is located within sight of the Celtic Sea, but from 1938 some

6,000 acres of land belonging to the Stackpole Estate was requisitioned by the Ministry of Defence to form a permanent military training area and today is fenced off, thereby denying the public access to the coast. For security and safety reasons, the Ministry has insisted that walkers are unexpectedly diverted, giving them no choice but to tread the hard surface of the B4319.

It will be recalled that in the north of the county, the Ministry of Defence were denied that opportunity through unyielding opposition in Preseli. The south of the county is rather different. It had previous experience of the military at Stackpole Court. A majestic edifice originally built in the 1730s, soldiers were once billeted here – until they destroyed it through stripping lead from its roof, causing dry and wet rot. The building was sadly demolished in 1963. The estate is today in the care of the National Trust and is a top attraction to tourists from all over the world.

The early 1960s witnessed a further military incursion, but of a very different kind to that previously mentioned, which went beyond the experience of the people of Pembrokeshire. In May to August of 1961, as part of a NATO arrangement, the community of Castlemartin saw the arrival of the German Army's 84th Panzer Division, who occupied 5,000 acres of land as part of a tank-training area. Some 84,000 troops passed through Castlemartin up until 1996, when – after the fall of the Berlin Wall – they relocated to East Germany.

This unusual invasion by German forces into an 'English' community in the 1960s initially caused outcry, with many recalling the events of 19 August 1940, when the German Luftwaffe bombed the oil storage depots at Llanreath in Pembroke Dock (Doc Penfro). When three German Junkers escorted by two Messerschmitt 109 fighters dropped their bombs, the fire caused was said to

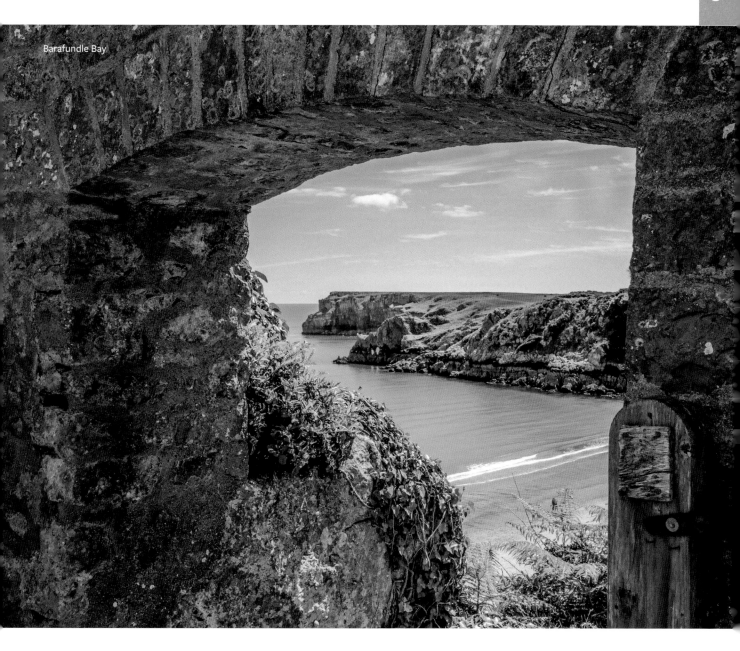

Barafundle Bay

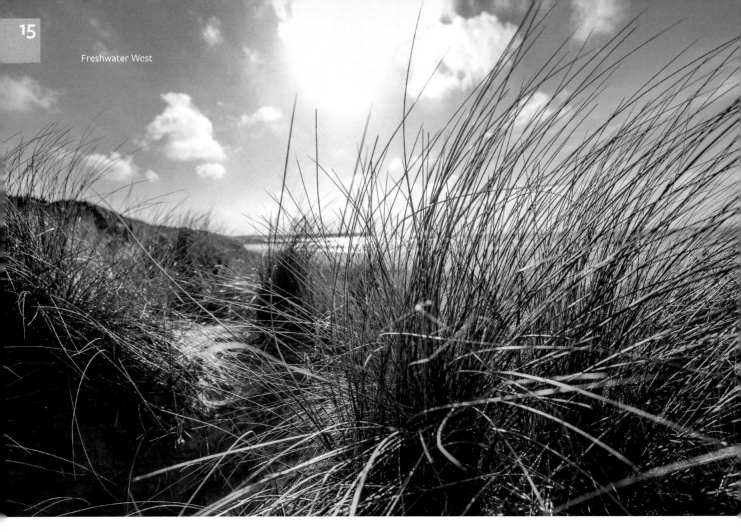

be the largest in Britain since the Great Fire of London in 1666. A direct hit caused 33 million gallons of oil to be destroyed, with the fire threatening to engulf the town. It took 650 firefighters three weeks to extinguish the blaze, with five from Cardiff losing their lives. That tragic conflagration caused by an invasion from the sky is still a local talking point. Pembroke Dock was also the home of the Sunderland Flying Boat, perhaps the largest

flying boat base in the world, to guard against attacks upon merchant convoys by German U-boat during the Battle of the Atlantic. It was therefore not surprising that that the county as a whole did not warm to yet another invasion. Initial xenophobia, however, was to give way to warmth, hospitality and mutual respect in the community. In fact, the German authorities helped to restore the ancient parish of Warren's medieval church of St Mary,

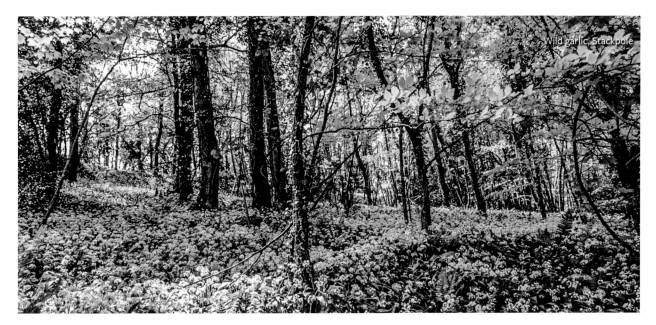
Wild garlic, Stackpole

dating from 1290, which bids a welcome/*willkommen* to both British and German forces who were once based at Castlemartin.

During training the guns can be heard all around the estate. Visitors to Bosherston Lily Ponds, and to areas of outstanding natural beauty far across the Cleddau Estuary, may be forgiven for thinking on occasion that the county is in the grip of a thunderstorm. Local inhabitants after dusk live through a perpetual meteor shower of night fire. The church of St Michael at Bosherston (Llanfihangel-clogwyn-Gofan), a typical Norman structure of the thirteenth century with a castellated tower, may typify the Anglo Norman influence in the south of the county but is at odds with the guns and tanks.

There is always the potential for loss of life to soldiers during training. There has recently been a three-pronged investigation by the Health and Safety Executive,

Dyfed Powys Police and the Ministry of Defence into an explosion which caused two fatalities and casualties amongst members of the Royal Tank Regiment at Castlemartin. In July 2018, a senior coroner found that the cause of the explosion was a design flaw, and that the gun had not been adequately tested during the manufacturing and production process. The fault lay with the designers and the Ministry of Defence.

With its Caribbean-like features, Barafundle Beach and Bay – voted one of the best beaches in Britain, and a serious contender on the world map – is a world away from such an unpleasant intrusion as the sound of guns. Thousands of tourists from all over the globe are attracted to this idyllic setting and back on the Pembrokeshire Coastal Path are oblivious to military presence, if only for a short time.

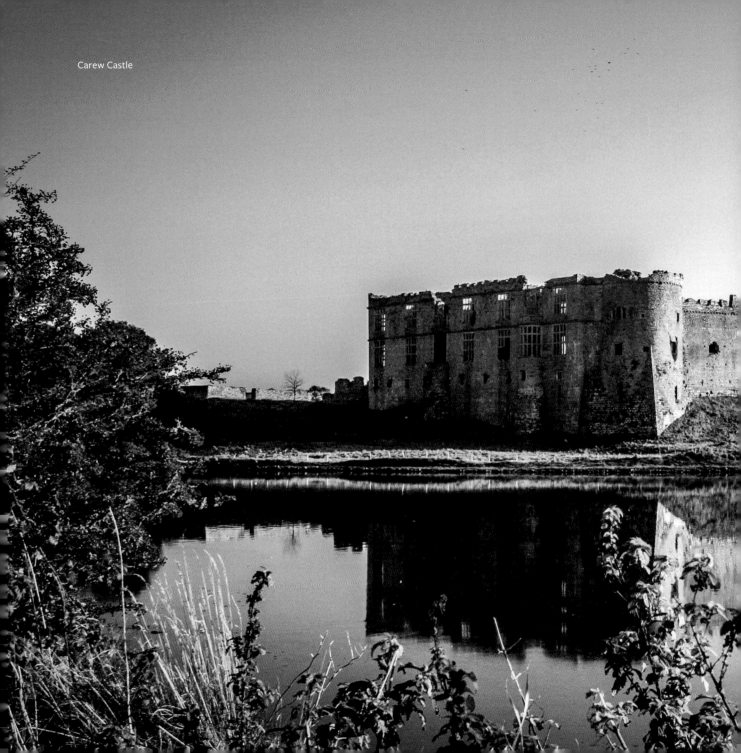

Carew Castle

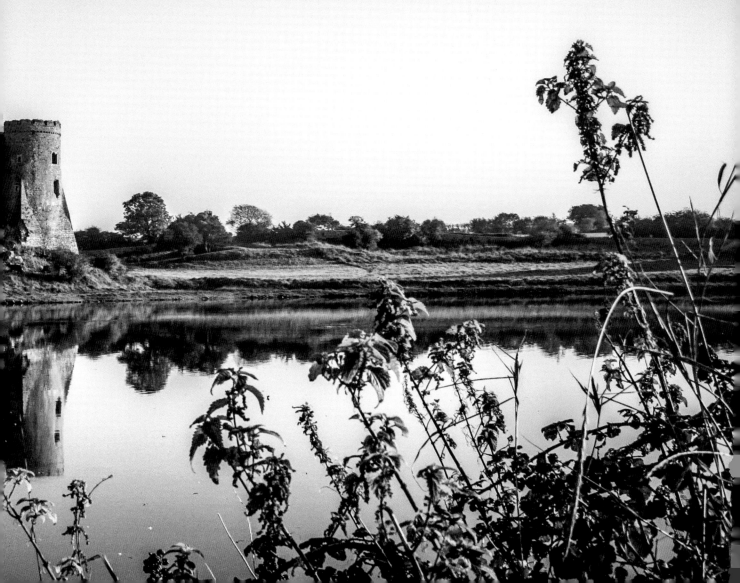

St Govan's, Manorbier and Carew

A disappointed contender to the see of St Davids, and the Pembrokeshire Commissioner for Piracy

AWAY FROM WAR games and any remaining opposition to the Ministry of Defence, there is a unique opportunity to descend upon a retreat which is rich in legend. St Govan's Chapel is hidden from the public eye beneath a cliff face near Bosherston (Llanfihangel-clogwyn-Gofan) known as St Govan's Head. Legend has it that Govan (Gofan) was an Irish monk who travelled to the county and was attacked by pirates, and thus sought refuge in the fissure in the cliff over which the thirteenth-century chapel now stands. Thereafter, he led a hermitic existence, catching fish and taking water from two springs nearby. Miraculously his handprints are allegedly still to be seen in the floor in a cave behind the chapel.

When I carefully descended the seemingly endless steps into the chapel, I could not help but be aware of the obvious peacefulness but also be alerted to the strong, acrid smell of cannabis. On peering out of the chapel window, I saw the source of the pungent aroma: two harmless students taking in not just the weed but also the striking rock formation as part of their curriculum. The Bell Rock at the water's edge supposedly houses Govan's silver bell, encased in the rock by angels to safeguard it from being stolen by returning pirates. An urban myth this may be, but the link with piracy is central to the story.

The majestic Manorbier Castle (Castell Maenorbŷr) was the original seat of the Anglo-Norman de Barry family and the birthplace of Giraldus Cambrensis (Gerald of Wales) in c.1146. Gerald was of mixed ancestry, being the son of a Norman and a direct descendant of Rhys ap Tewdwr, the last King of Deheubarth. In 1176, Gerald was nominated as Bishop of St Davids but his appointment to the see was blocked by Henry II of England, possibly because of his partial Welsh heritage and his link to the ruling family of Deheubarth. Gerald claimed that the King had said, "Such an appointment would only give strength to the Welsh and increase their pride."

The rectangular, enclosed castle, standing strategically overlooking the bay, dominates the village. The castle is built on a natural promontory and has a postern gate, built inconspicuously, that secretly provides access to the beach and boats. It was believed to be a safe haven for looted plunder – little wonder with its fortification and ease of access to the sea. The British film industry once more saw an opportunity for a film set with this outstanding backdrop: *I Capture the Castle* with Bill Nighy, released in 2003, was partly shot at Manorbier Castle. This outstanding site overlooks beaches that can only be accessed on foot or from the sea, and was considered to be a vantage point for smugglers. Across the valley is the Church of St James, with its conspicuous white tower.

The surrounding area, particularly the rock formation at Church Doors on the Lydstep peninsula, is a paradise to any visiting geologist. Sidestepping a prominent MOD notice warning that the path is in the vicinity of a missile firing range, the long descent leads unexpectedly to exciting caverns and a deep smugglers' cove.

Travelling inland, you soon reach the magnificent Carew Castle (Castell Caeriw) and Tidal Mill, boasting an interesting historical background. Towards the end of the eleventh century, the Normans furthered their

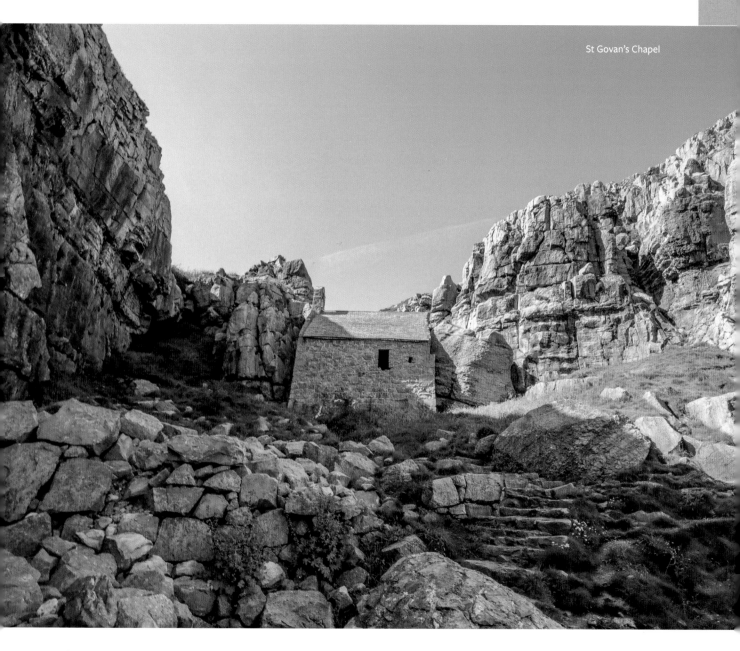

St Govan's Chapel

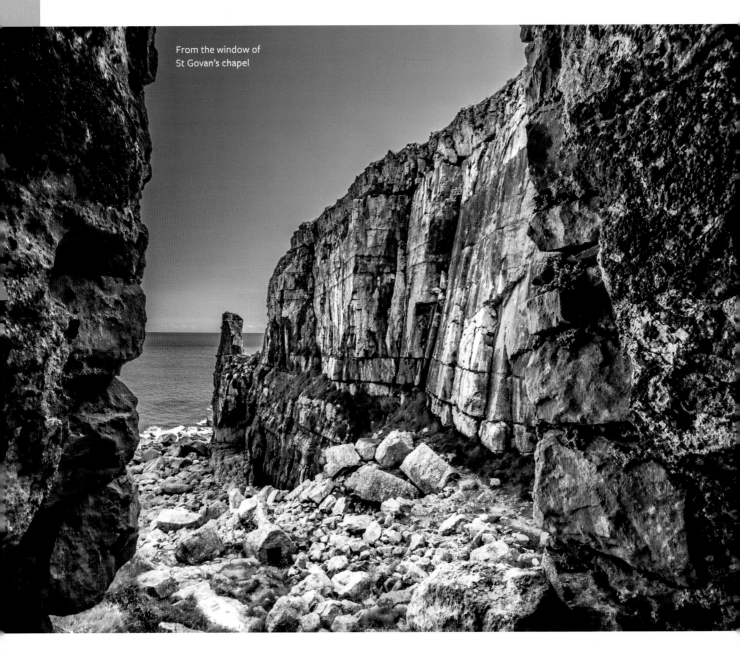

From the window of
St Govan's chapel

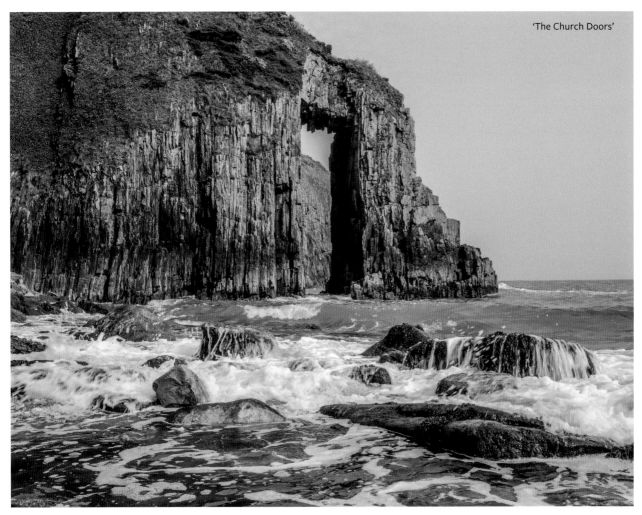

'The Church Doors'

conquest when they invaded Wales and made Pembroke Castle (Castell Penfro) the heart of their dominance in the county. Carew is but a few miles away. At the site of Carew Castle there was once a Roman fort built by earlier invaders, which was later developed by Sir Nicholas de Carew (who died in 1311). Sir Rhys ap Thomas (1449–1525), who played a significant role in the victory of Henry Tudor at Bosworth, later took residence there, and later again it became the home of Sir John Perrott.

Perrott (1528–1592) was once reputed to be the illegitimate son of Henry VIII. The credibility of his connection to Henry is debatable, though it has a certain

Manorbier Castle

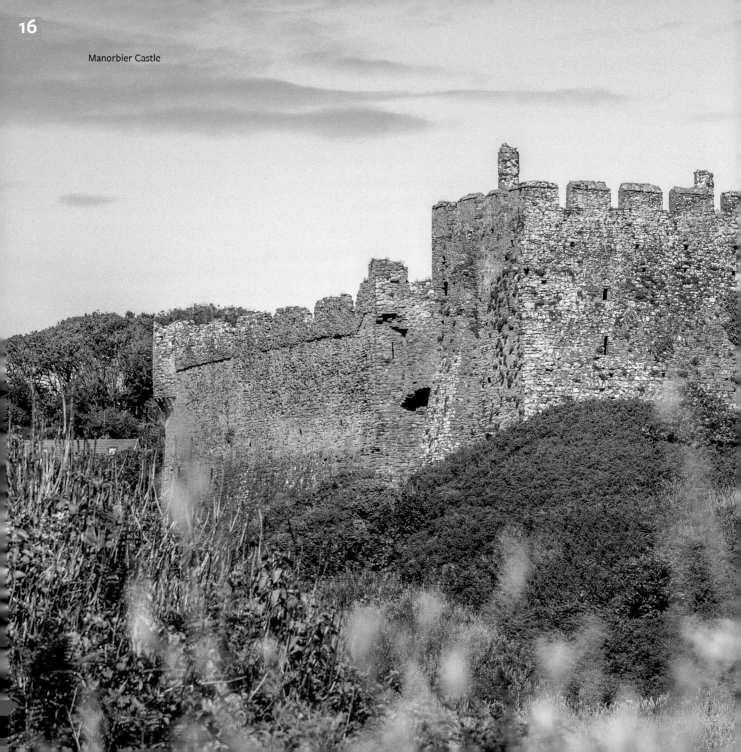

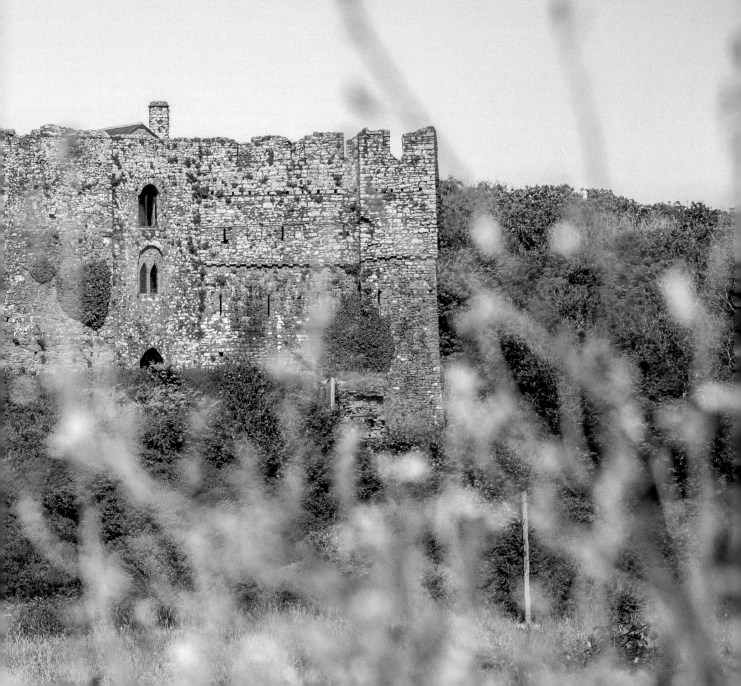

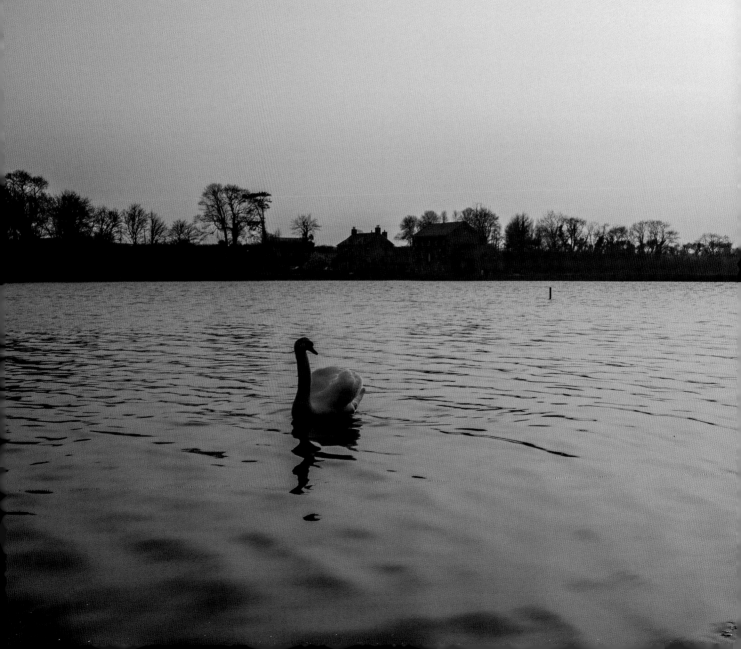

Carew Tidal Mill

appeal to romantics. However, the Tudor link with Pembroke did serve him well, as he was appointed Lord Deputy to Queen Elizabeth I during the conquest of Ireland.

In 1578 Perrott was the subject of accusations involving piracy and assisting the activities of smugglers off the Welsh coast, having allegedly become involved with a gang of pirates who captured a vessel off Milford Haven (Aberdaugleddau) containing a cargo of salt that came into his possession. Despite this, he retained the confidence of the Crown, and later the same year was appointed Commissioner for Piracy in Pembrokeshire and given command of a naval squadron guarding the Irish Coast from Spanish invasion. Unfortunately his gentrified existence at Carew Castle came to an end when he was arrested for treason and later died in the Tower of London.

Another attractive feature, alien to the architecture of the county but linked to the castle and the Carew family, is the French Tidal Mill and causeway – the only restored tidal mill in Wales. The use of French burr stone in the grinding process is its notable feature.

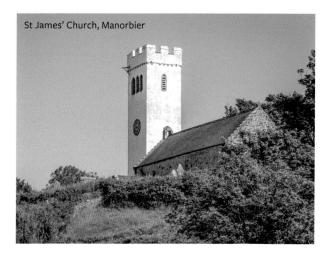

St James' Church, Manorbier

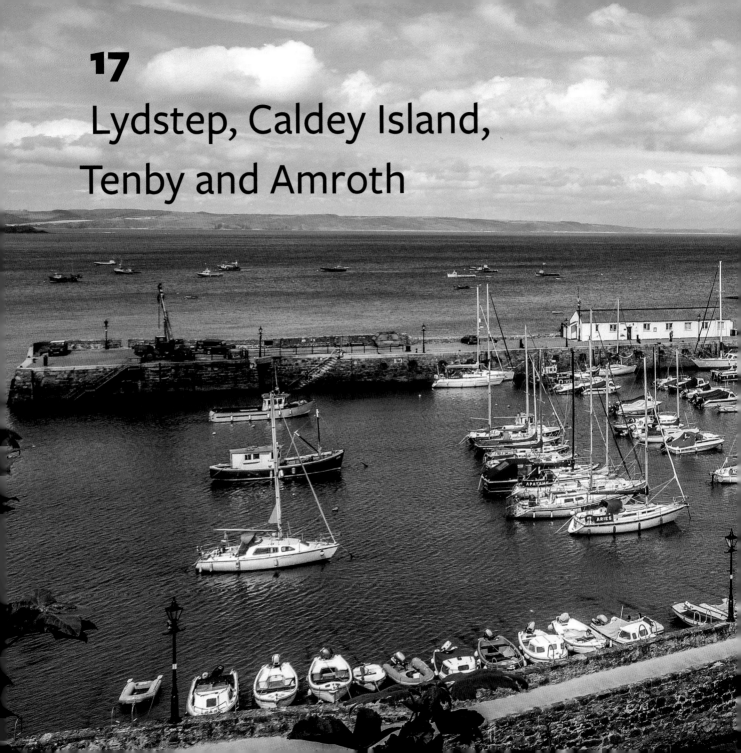

17

Lydstep, Caldey Island, Tenby and Amroth

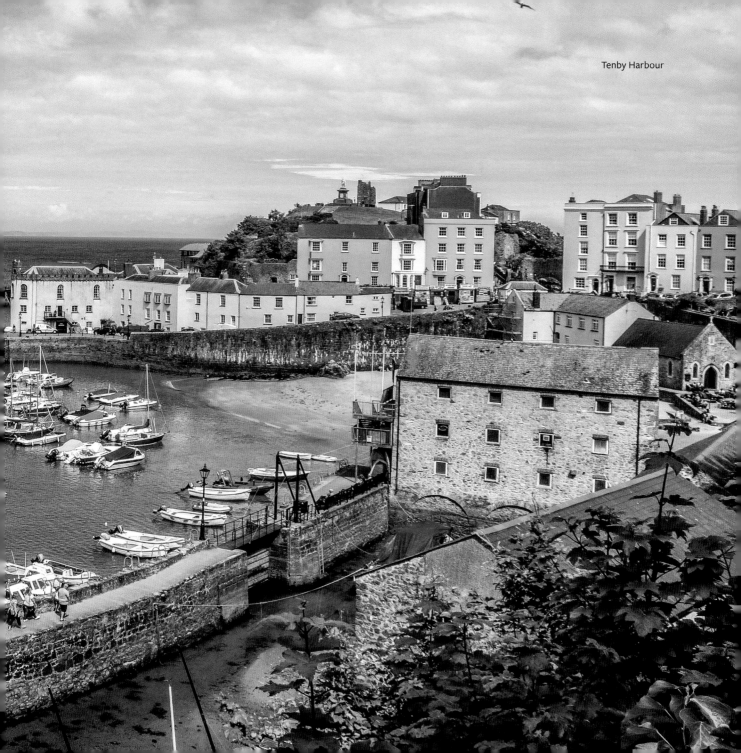
Tenby Harbour

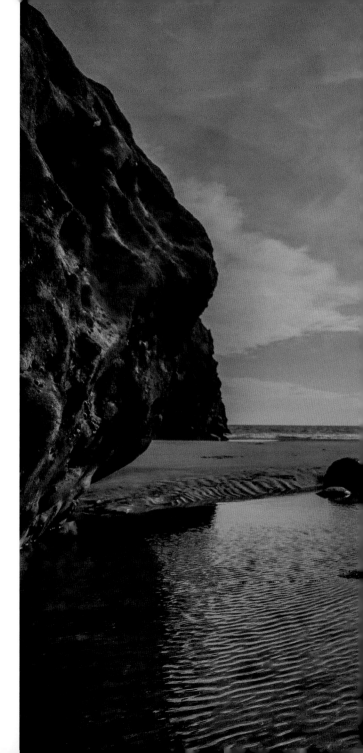

The tourist invasion, a benefit gained from opium, and the Allied landings

FOLLOWING THE COAST overlooking Carmarthen Bay (Bae Caerfyrddin), the vista is impressive as the eye focuses on what some would contend are the best beaches that the county has to offer. Lydstep Caverns and other picturesque coves, coupled with magnificent cliffs and rock formations, together with a micro-climate that escapes the blustery wet weather drifting over from Ireland, makes the area a much sought-after tourist destination. Thousands of visitors arrive from March through to November. The business community welcomes this annual invasion with open arms, only to then hanker for the solitude that the dark winter months have to offer. This commercial element dominating the area is not as prevalent in the coastal regions north of the Landsker, where the seascape is equally attractive and where tourists visit for different reasons.

Caldey Island (Ynys Bŷr) is conspicuous for its lighthouse cutting across the skyline, looking towards Carmarthen Bay. Nestling here is a tranquil Cistercian monastery and the thirteenth-century church of St Illtud, its spire just visible to the naked eye from the south beach at Tenby (Dinbych-y-pysgod). Seafarers in years gone by regarded Caldey with its hidden coves as a safe haven for stashing their plunder.

Scottish-born John Paul Jones (1747–1792), though the United States' first well-known naval commander and sometimes referred to as 'the father of the US Navy', was allegedly a marauding pirate. He had a connection with

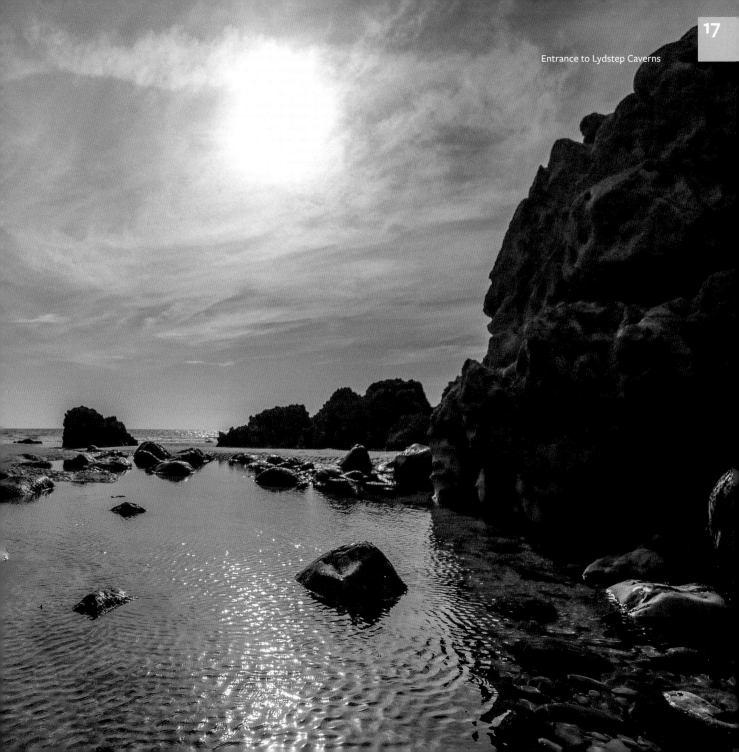

Entrance to Lydstep Caverns

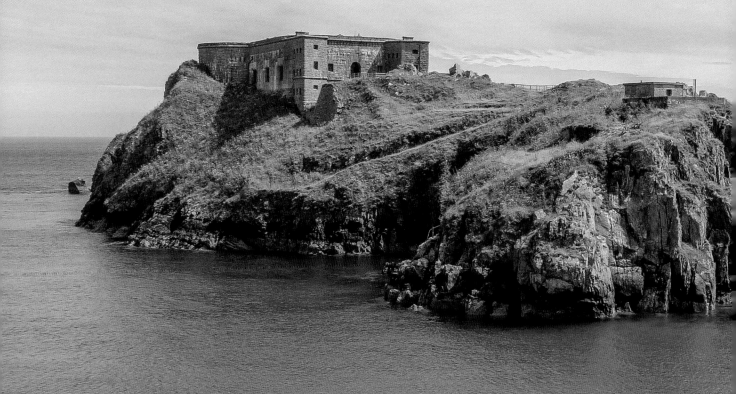

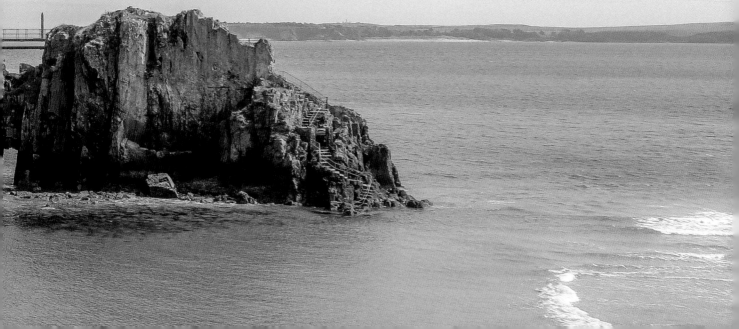

St Catherine's Island looking towards Caldey Island

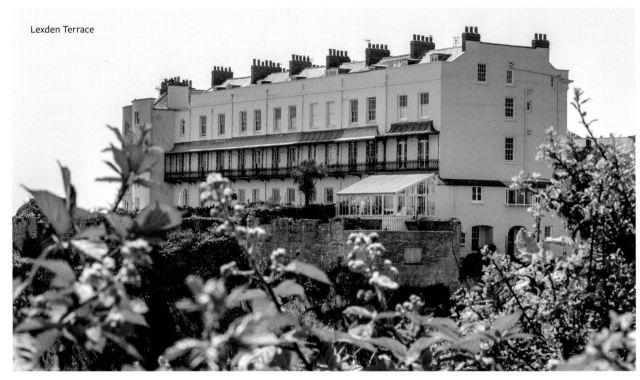

Lexden Terrace

Caldey Island, where he would take on fresh water at what is now known as Paul Jones Bay, in the north-east of the island. Legend has it that his body is buried on Caldey, in a crevice at Ord Point. His accomplice was a seafarer from Tenby who went by the unusual name of Leekie Porridge.

Sir Henry Morgan (1635–1688), renowned buccaneer born in Llanrumney, Cardiff (Caerdydd), was also no stranger to Caldey Island. He began his career as a privateer sailing the Caribbean, and later became Lieutenant Governor of Jamaica, but was reputed to have links with Pembrokeshire, hiding his plunder on Caldey Island before docking on the mainland.

As well as spoils of gold and silver, valuable cargoes of whisky, tobacco and spices were also of particular interest to local inhabitants, whether for personal consumption or onward sale. Vast quantities were apparently secreted in the Cathedral Caves on Caldey Island, such commodities being brought ashore from shipwrecks.

Tenby, with its picturesque harbour, endless beaches and an eclectic mix of Regency, late Georgian and Victorian architecture as a backdrop, attracts tourists for obvious reasons. Behind some of these facades lies a wealth of historical material disguising smuggling and piracy – and in one particular instance, on an unprecedented scale.

Lexden Terrace, built in 1843 on St Julian Street and claimed by architectural historians as 'Tenby's finest terrace', was built for Captain John Rees. Born in Tenby, he amassed considerable wealth, principally through trading in opium. Though it was universally accepted as an effective medicine at the time, it was illegal in China, where addiction was widespread. Trafficking opium through smugglers between Calcutta and the coast of China provided him with a golden opportunity for enrichment. His productive trade in opium ended before China attempted to suppress sale of the narcotic, leading to the first Opium War of 1840. Having reaped the benefit of his piratical activities, he was able to retire to Tenby and finance the building of the prestigious Grade II-listed Georgian terrace with the proceeds. Despite being one of the most prolific smugglers of opium in history, he was later to become a magistrate, an upstanding member of the local chapel and a philanthropist. In the Criminal Justice System of today, Captain John Rees would probably have been the subject of a Proceeds of Crime Investigation, and the 'benefit' that had accrued from his smuggling operations, namely Lexden Terrace, would in all likelihood have been declared an asset available for confiscation on behalf of the Crown.

In 2007, the cast and crew of the controversial film *The Edge of Love*, directed by John Maybury, descended for two days on Lexden House. The biopic about Dylan Thomas used the attractive location to shoot a raunchy bedroom scene involving the love triangle of Dylan (Matthew Rhys), Caitlin (Sienna Miller) and Vera Phillips (Keira Knightley).

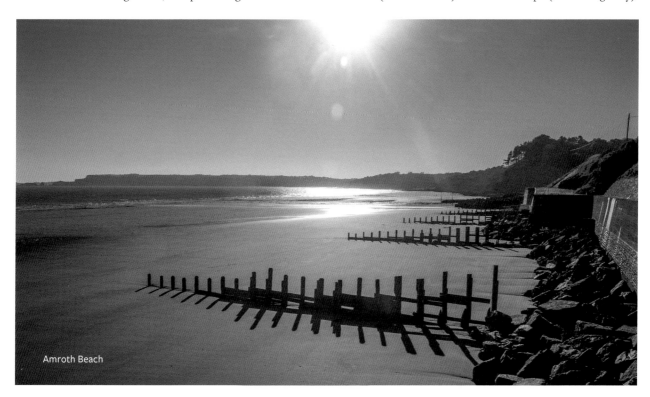

Amroth Beach

The 1998 BBC drama *Vanity Fair* was also filmed here.

Situated across the bay from Tenby's Castle Beach is St Catherine's Island (Ynys Catrin), another example of a late Victorian fort, purpose-built to guard against a naval threat from the sea. This was an extension of the Palmerston defence strategy seen surrounding the entrance to Milford Haven (Aberdaugleddau).

The summer of 1943 witnessed the arrival of a completely different variety of 'visitor', this time en bloc. Exercise Jantzen saw up to 100,000 men and landing craft shipped onto the beaches at Amroth, Wiseman's Bridge, Tenby and Saundersfoot (Llanussyllt) as part of a rehearsal for the amphibious D-Day Landings that took place on 6 June 1944. Over 16,000 tons of stores and ordnance were landed. The area, with its long beaches, had a similar terrain to Gold Beach in Normandy and the weather experienced during rehearsals was similar to that in Northern France.

In October 1943, over 5,000 American soldiers from the 110th US Infantry Regiment, part of the larger 28th US Infantry Division, were based at Llanion Barracks, Pembroke Dock (Doc Penfro) and across Pembrokeshire. Locals would attend dances at Cresselly House, enjoying their jives and jitterbugs with GIs. On 1 April 1944, the Supreme Allied Commander General Dwight D Eisenhower paid a surprise visit to the 110th regiment while the Prime Minister Winston Churchill and Admiral Viscount Mountbatten observed invasion exercises on the beaches of Amroth and Wiseman's Bridge. A memorial plaque commemorating the African-American servicemen who trained for D-Day in the county was unveiled at the World War II museum in the Control Tower at the former RAF base at Carew Cheriton on the 75th anniversary of D-Day.

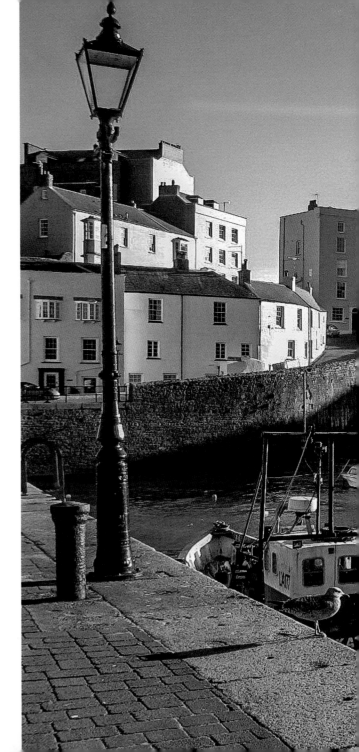

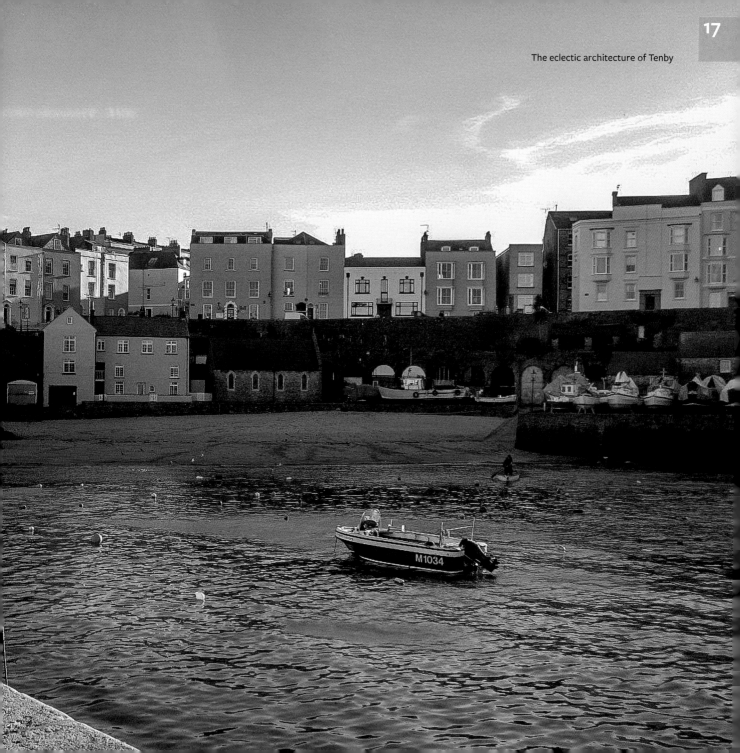

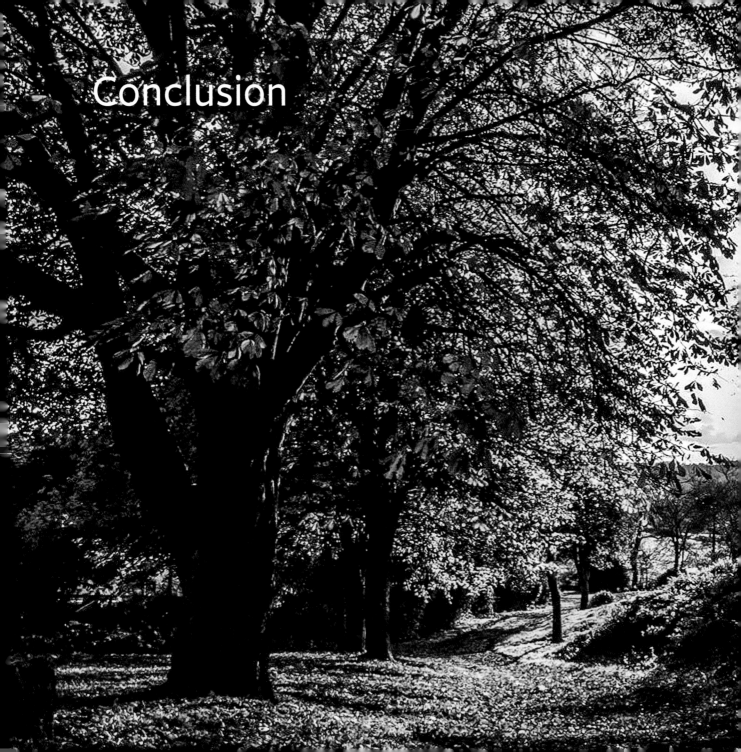

Conclusion

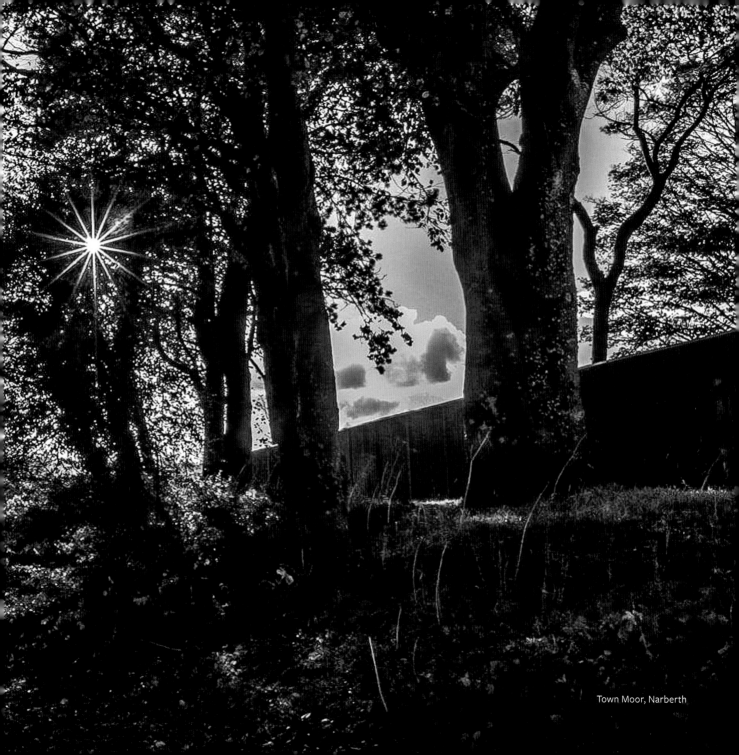

Town Moor, Narberth

THE PHOTOS AND anecdotes in this book are designed to breathe life into significant episodes in the changing face of this premier of counties. Through them, I hope to enrich the understanding of those readers who perhaps, until now, have not fully appreciated quite how important this little corner of Wales is, and has been, on the world stage.

I am conscious that my medley of milestones in its history is subjective and my passing commentary about some of the most controversial issues that have beset environmentalists and planners is essentially slanted. It is not intended to be contentious. Whilst some of these episodes are threadbare through the telling and others perhaps not so well known, I ask for a measure of tolerance. This is not designed to be a comprehensive history of Pembrokeshire. Likewise, I have not attempted to cover every single step of the way, travelling from north to south, either side of the Landsker Line.

In the last couple of years we have witnessed a real sea-change in attitude towards history, especially where this is in some way connected to slavery, ethnicity, the rights of minority groups and fundamental human freedoms. I fully support these concerns, and while they were not in the forefront of my mind when writing, I sincerely hope that nothing that I have included will cause offence.

It also goes without saying that the advent of a global pandemic has had a universal and profound effect upon business and tourism, and their future remains very much unclear.

It is to be hoped that matters will quickly improve and that Pembrokeshire may continue to be a county of discovery and an environmental retreat. Vigilance and common sense must prevail if it is to remain so.

I hope you derive as much pleasure from looking through the images in the preceding pages as I have experienced in returning to those memorable locations and recapturing just some of the spectacular scenery of the county. If you are captivated by some of the historical detail included and wish to research matters in more depth, then so much the better.

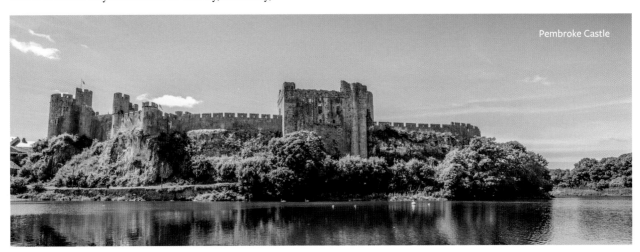
Pembroke Castle

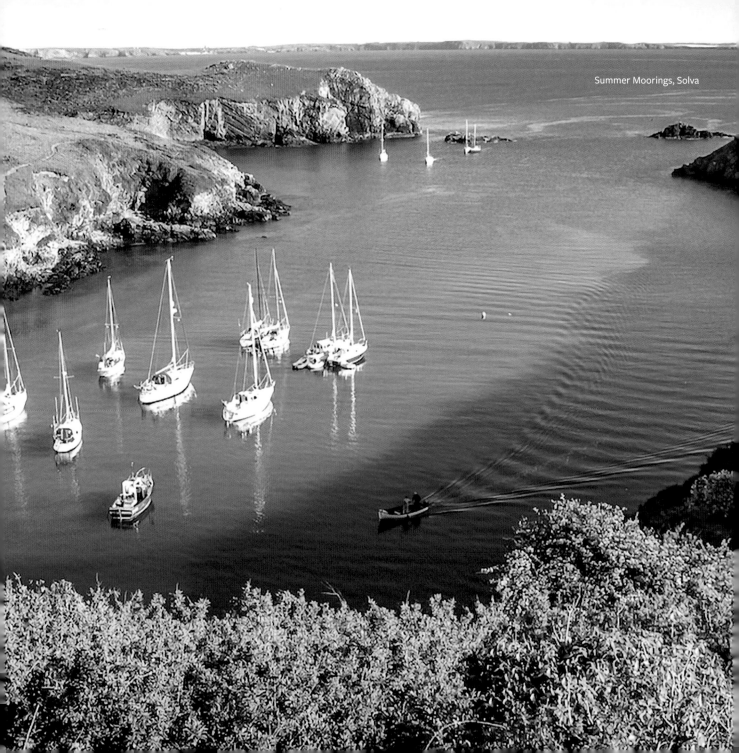
Summer Moorings, Solva

Acknowledgements

I OWE A particular debt of gratitude to my late parents, who inspired me to achieve academic and professional success. From an early age they instilled in me the importance of focusing on study whilst at school, listening to others, thinking for myself and speaking clearly. At times this code of conduct was abandoned when my endless appetite for playing lead guitar in a Sixties rock group and initial thoughts of going to art college conflicted with those values. After quickly waking up to reality and putting those bohemian pursuits aside, I acted upon that invaluable parental advice, and to considerable benefit, found my vocation in Law.

I am very much indebted to the author and playwright Gareth Miles, who provided the inspiration for this book, who looked over my work and caused me to revisit some of my provisional thoughts and to reshape some of my ideas. He also introduced me to the dynamic Welsh printing and publishing company, Y Lolfa.

I am forever grateful to Carolyn Hodges, my editor at Y Lolfa, who has tirelessly helped me throughout this work and curtailed my innate tendency towards verboseness.

If you have enjoyed the photography in this book, do check out my website:

http://www.iantomor-photography.co.uk.

Ieuan Morris
June 2021

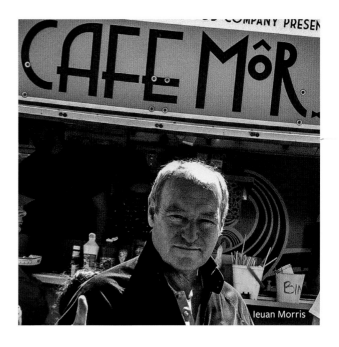

Ieuan Morris

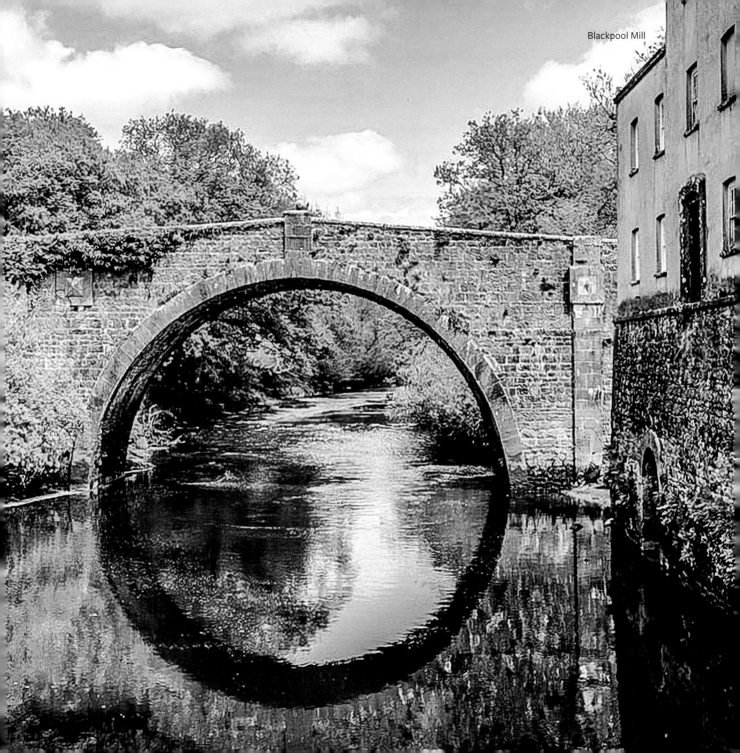

Blackpool Mill

Also from Y Lolfa:

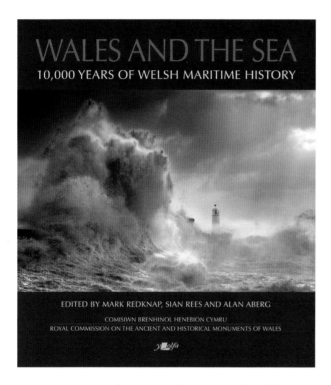

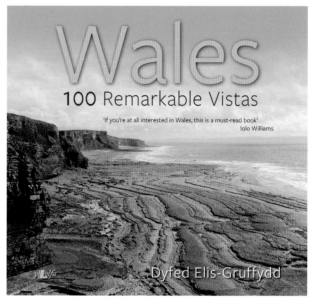

An extremely comprehensive book with hundreds of colour photos, presenting the whole of Wales' maritime history.

£24.99

A richly illustrated full-colour volume, taking readers on a journey around 100 of the most remarkable scenic locations in Wales.

£19.99

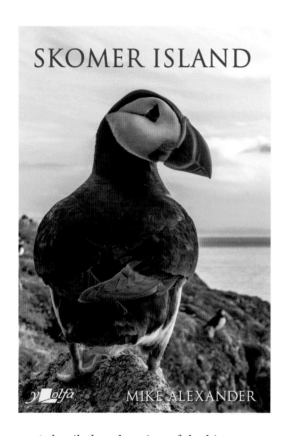

A detailed exploration of the history, landscape and wildlife of an incredibly special island. Packed with hundreds of breathtaking colour photos.

£29.99

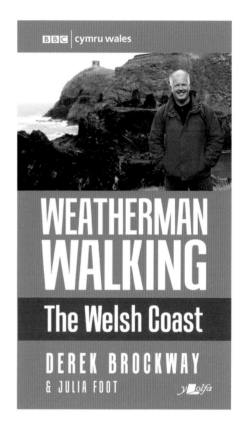

15 guided walks along the Wales Coast Path, as undertaken by Derek Brockway in BBC TV's 12th series of *Weatherman Walking*.

£9.99

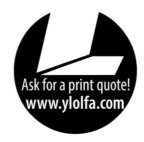